Giant Book Of Staff Paper For Mountain Dulcimer

Richard A. Ash

Copyright © 2013 Folkcraft Instruments, Inc.

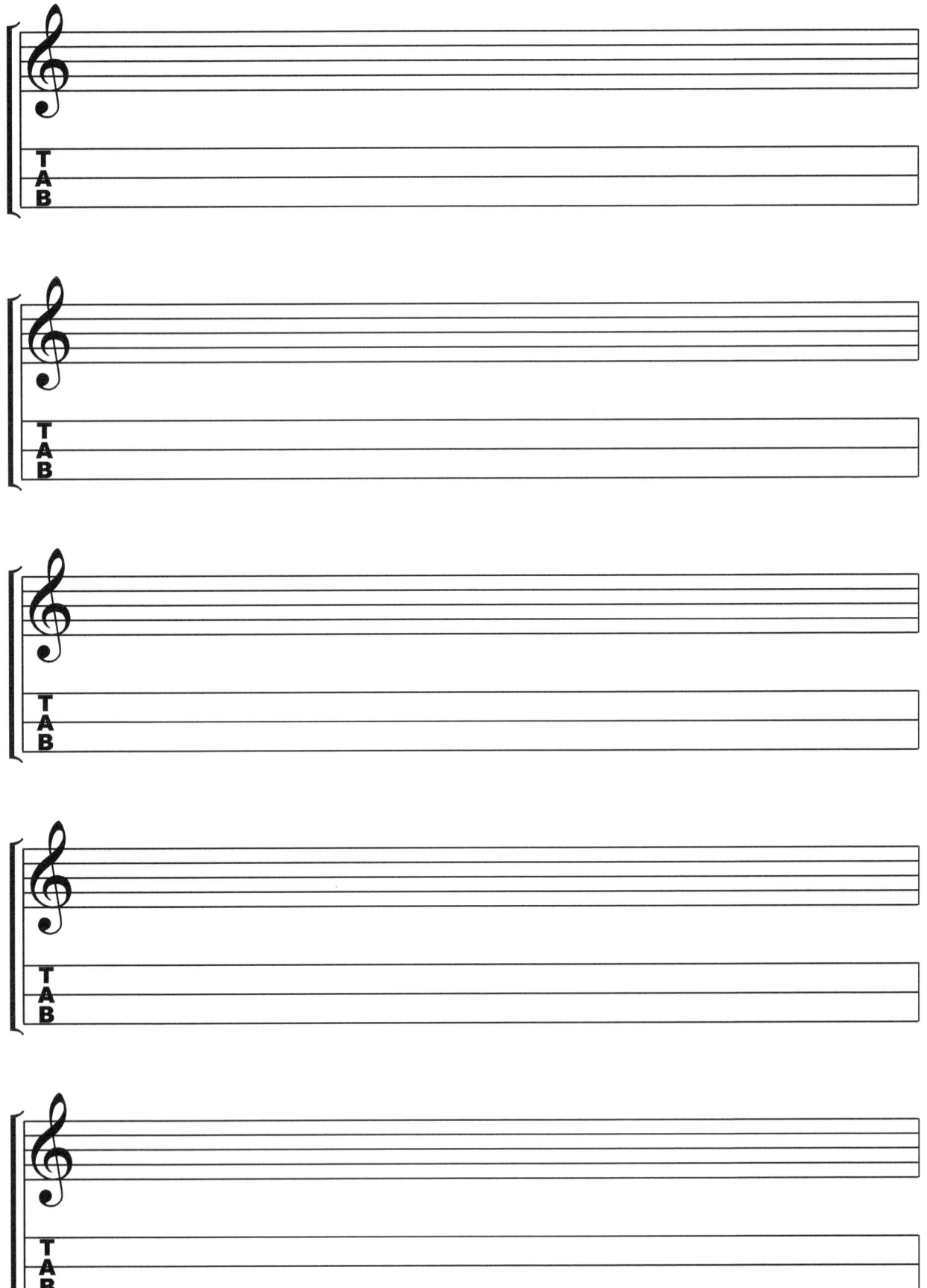

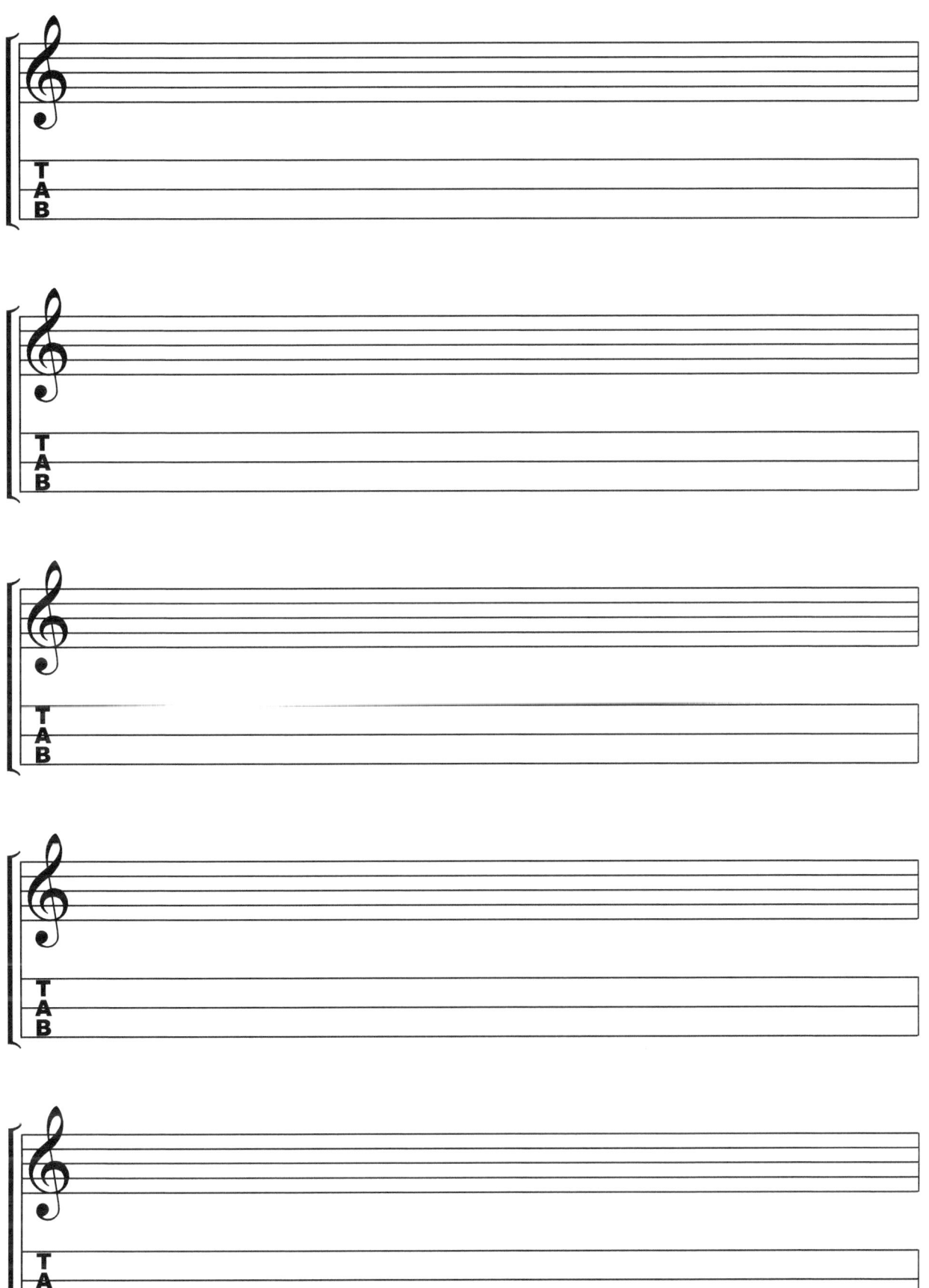

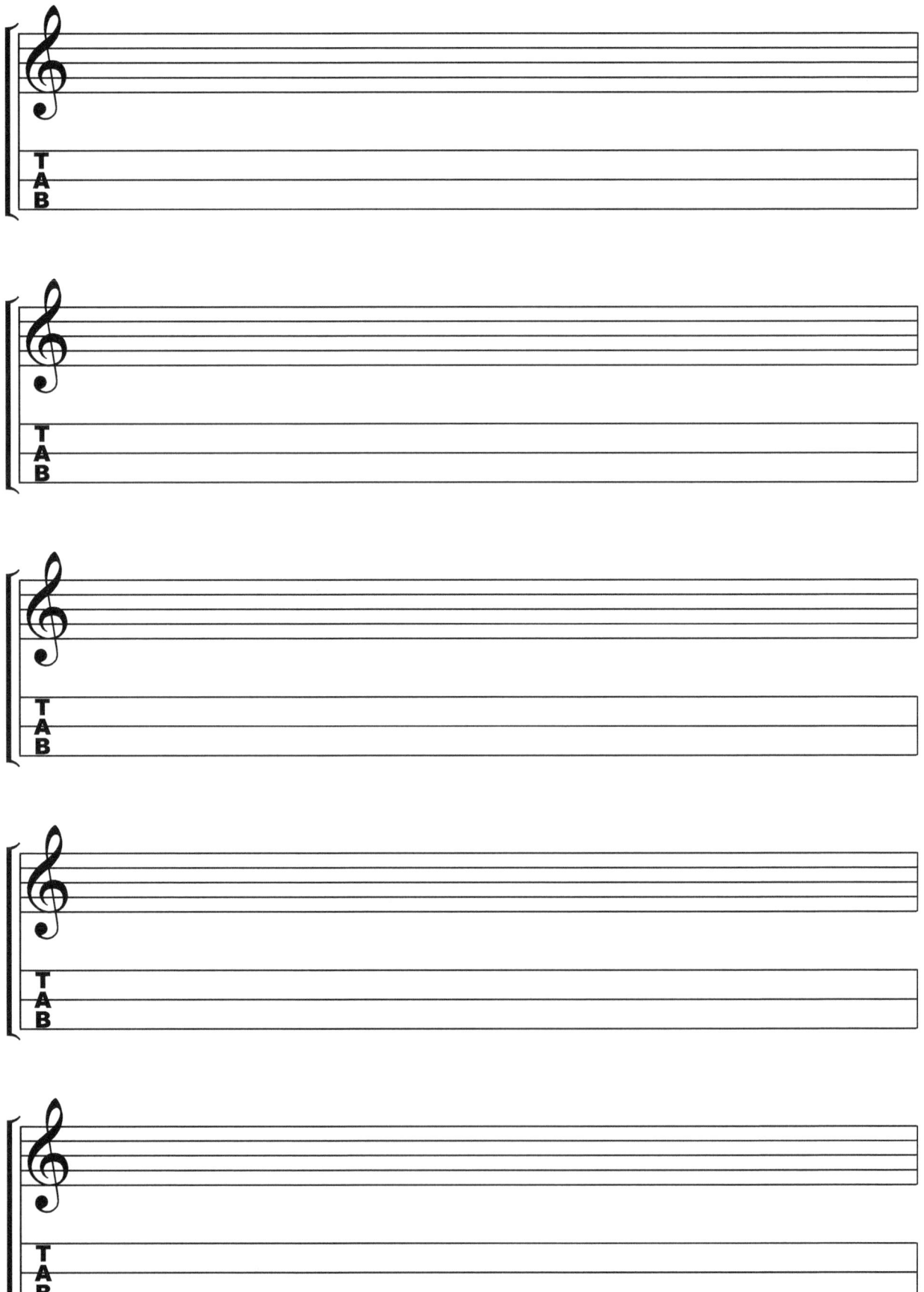

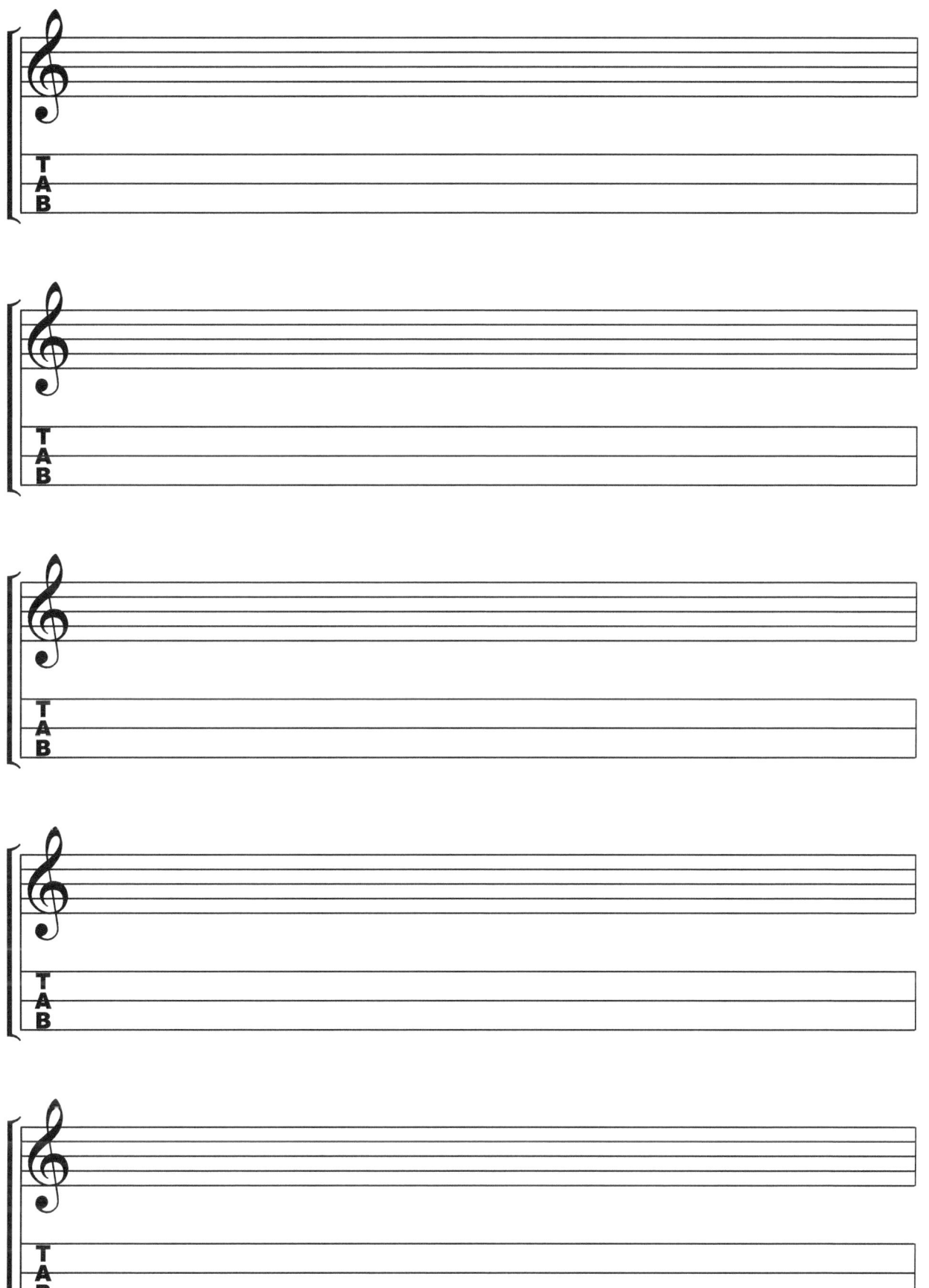

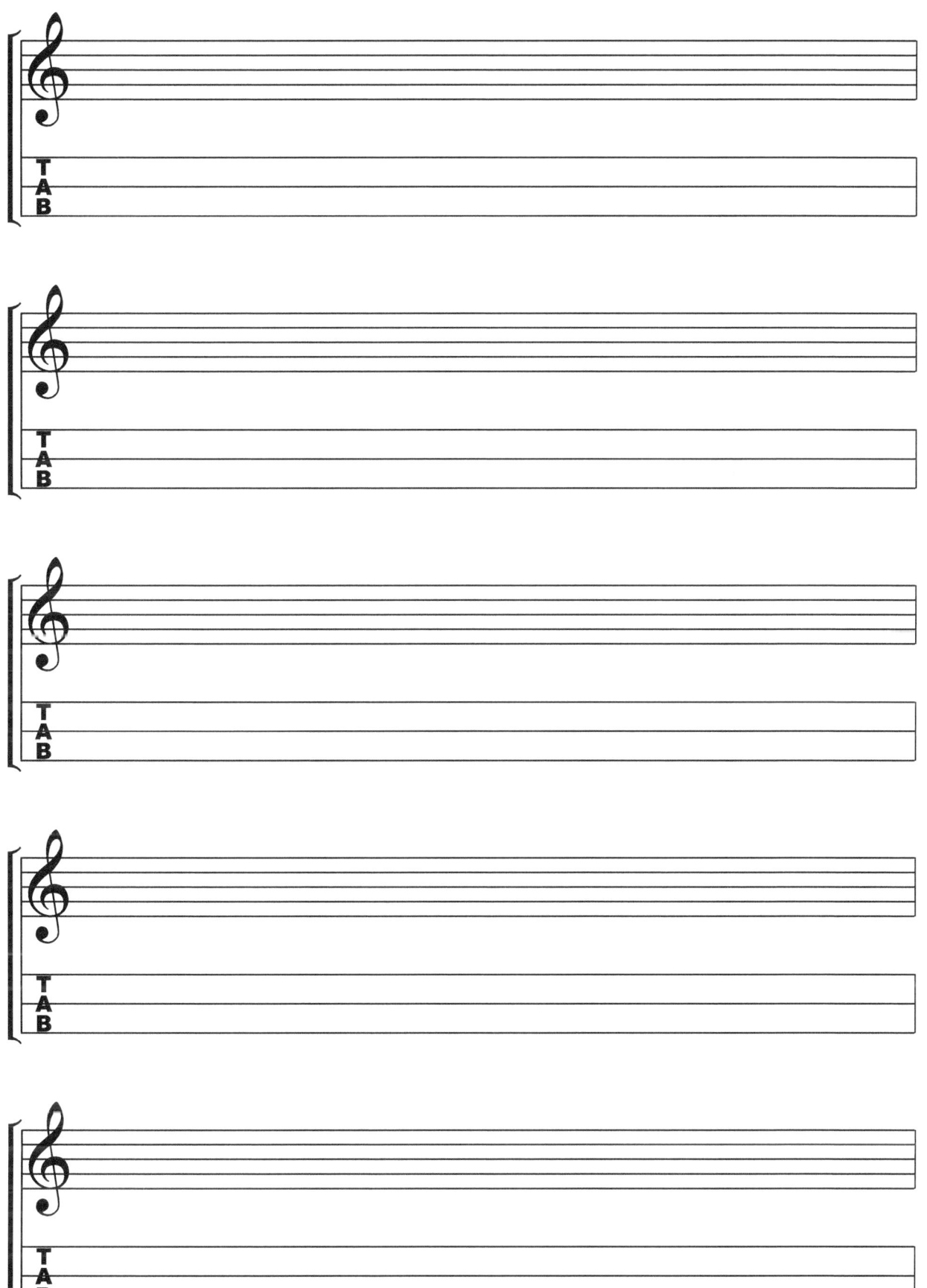

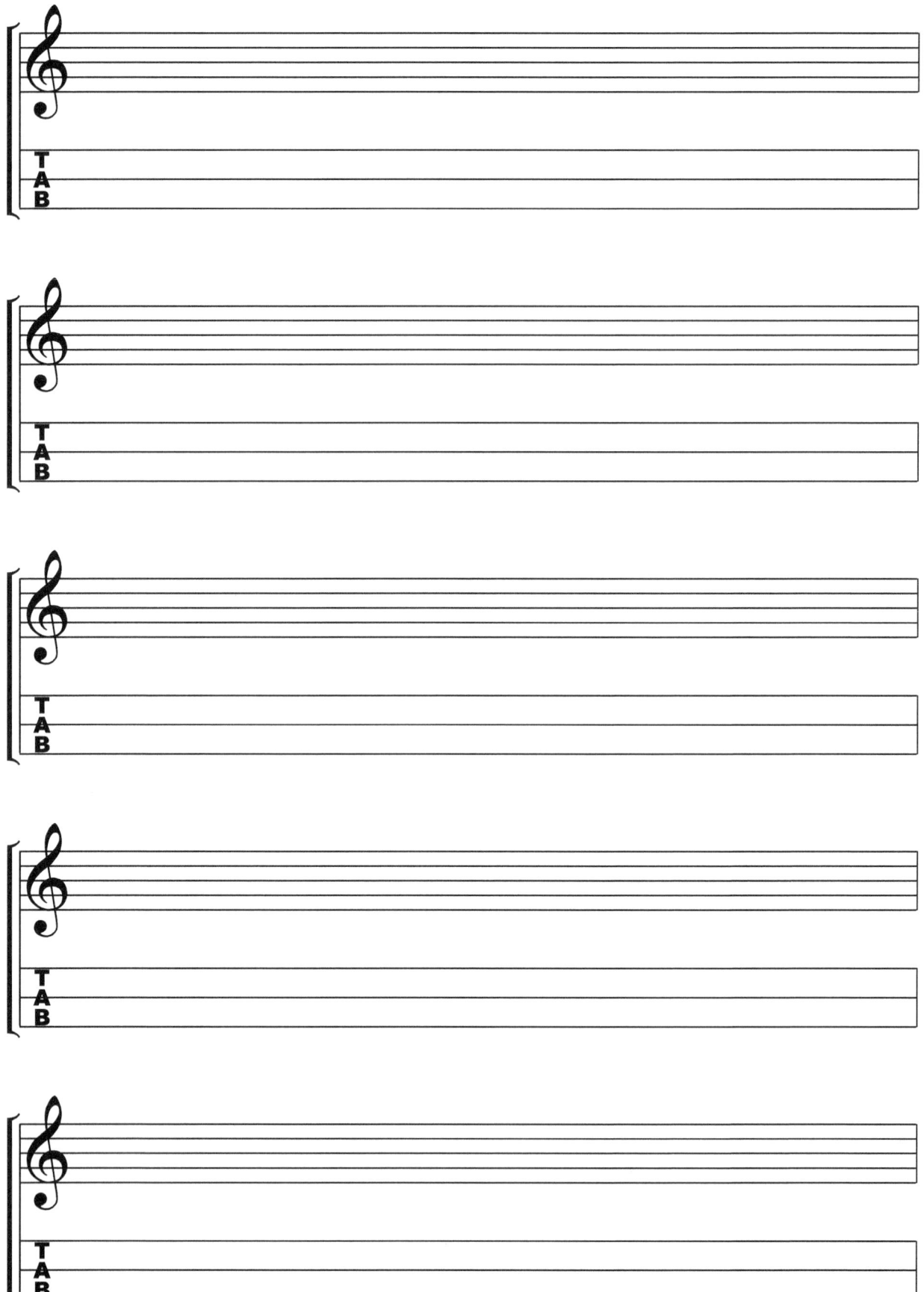

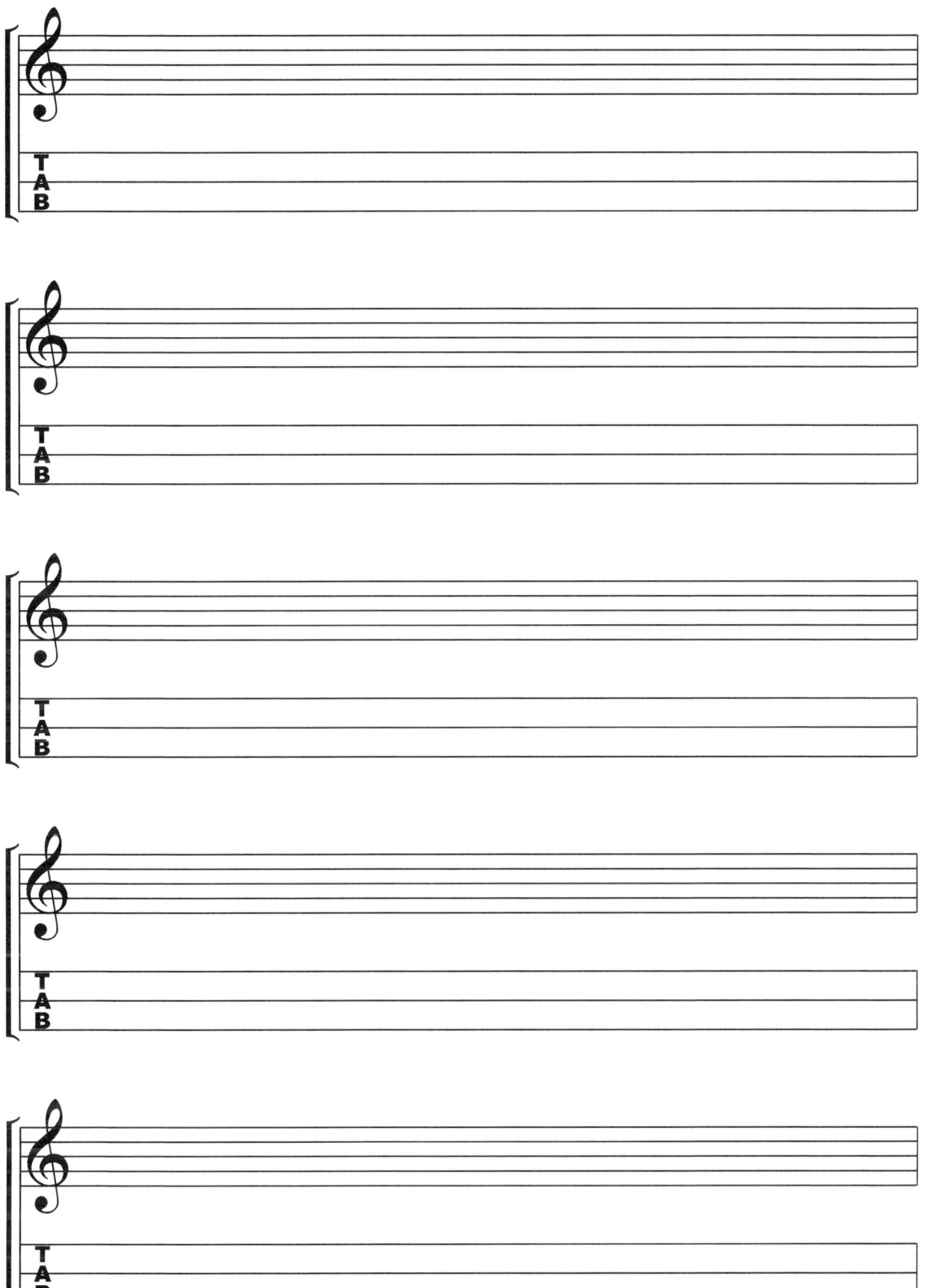

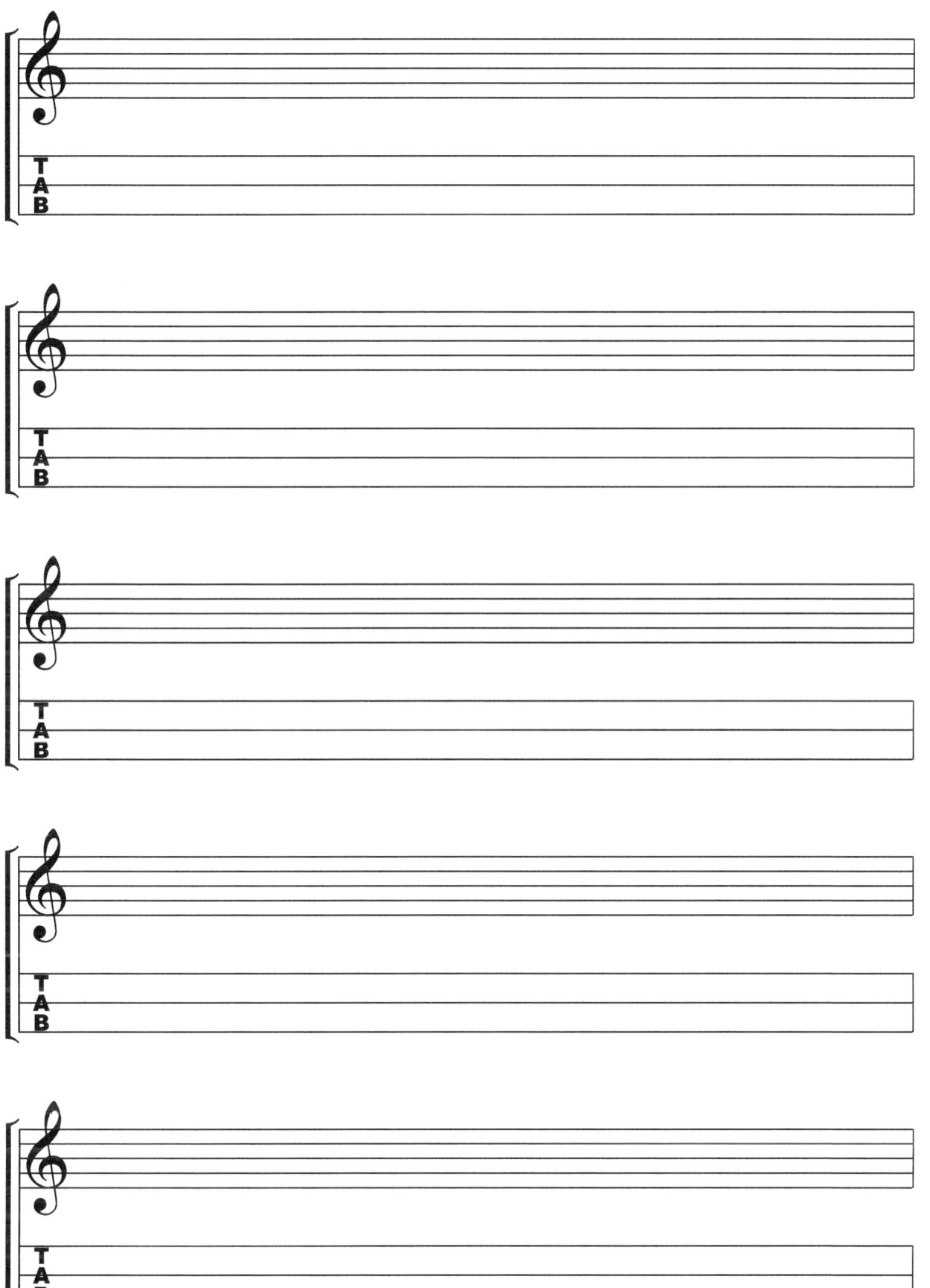

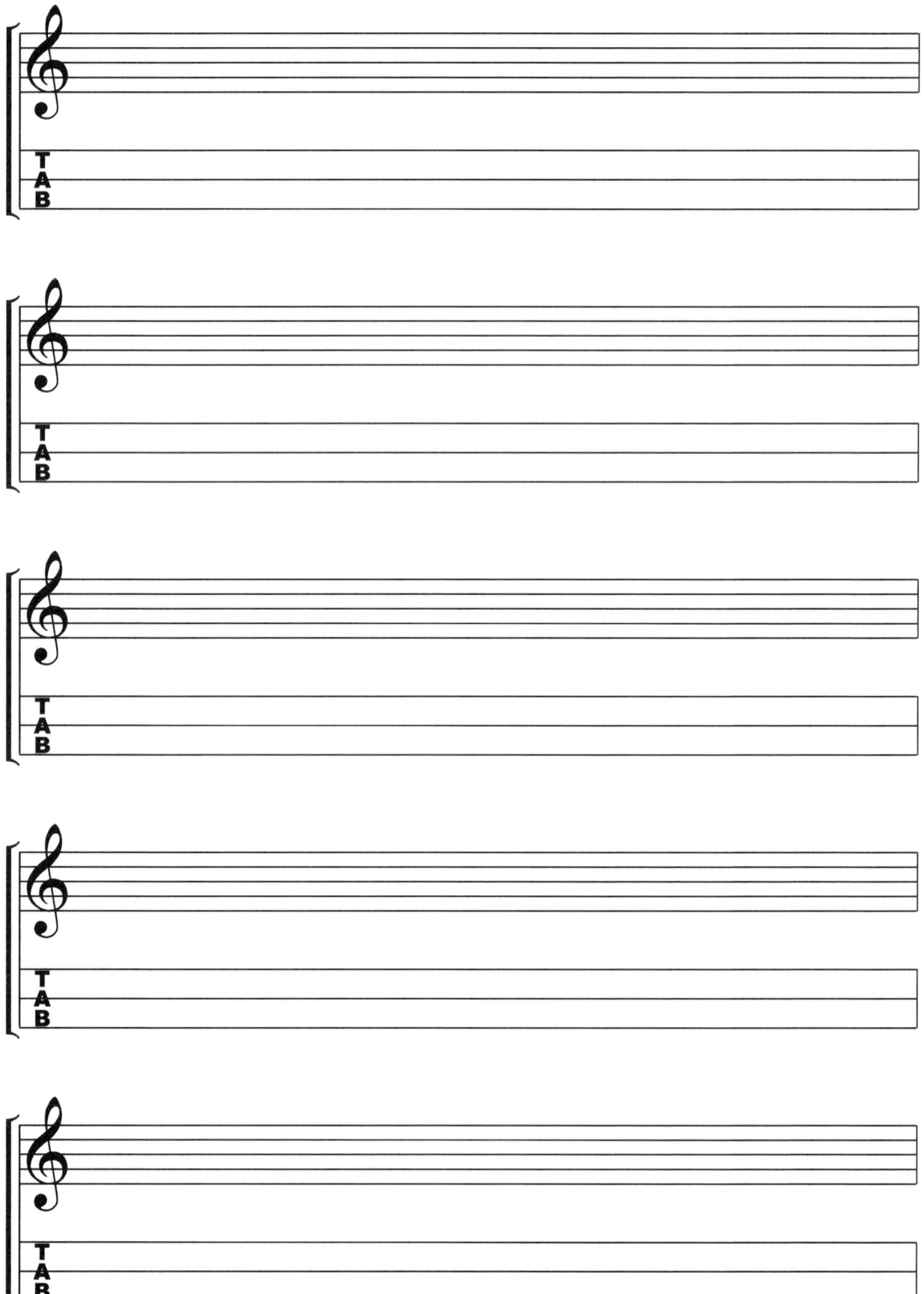

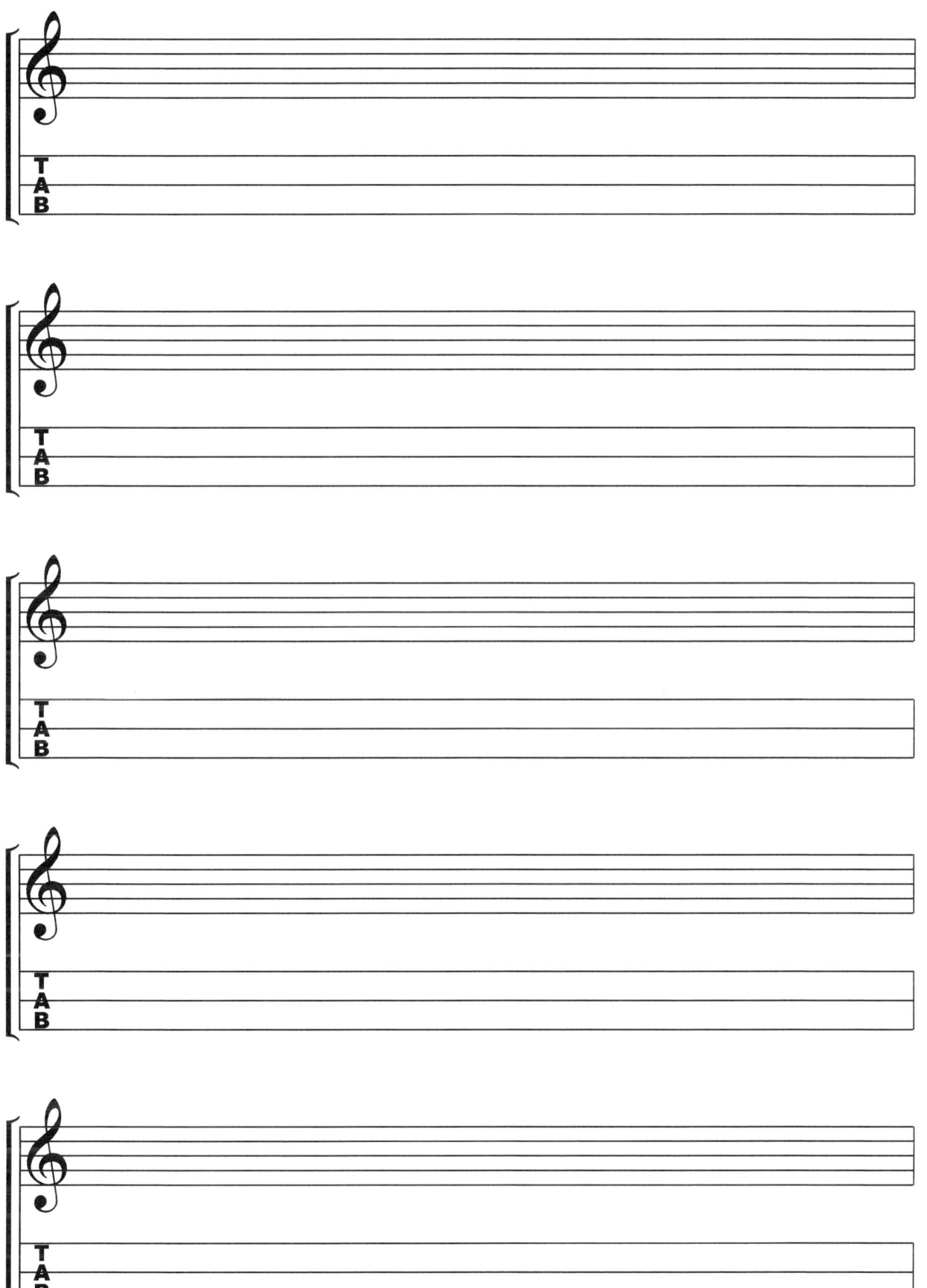

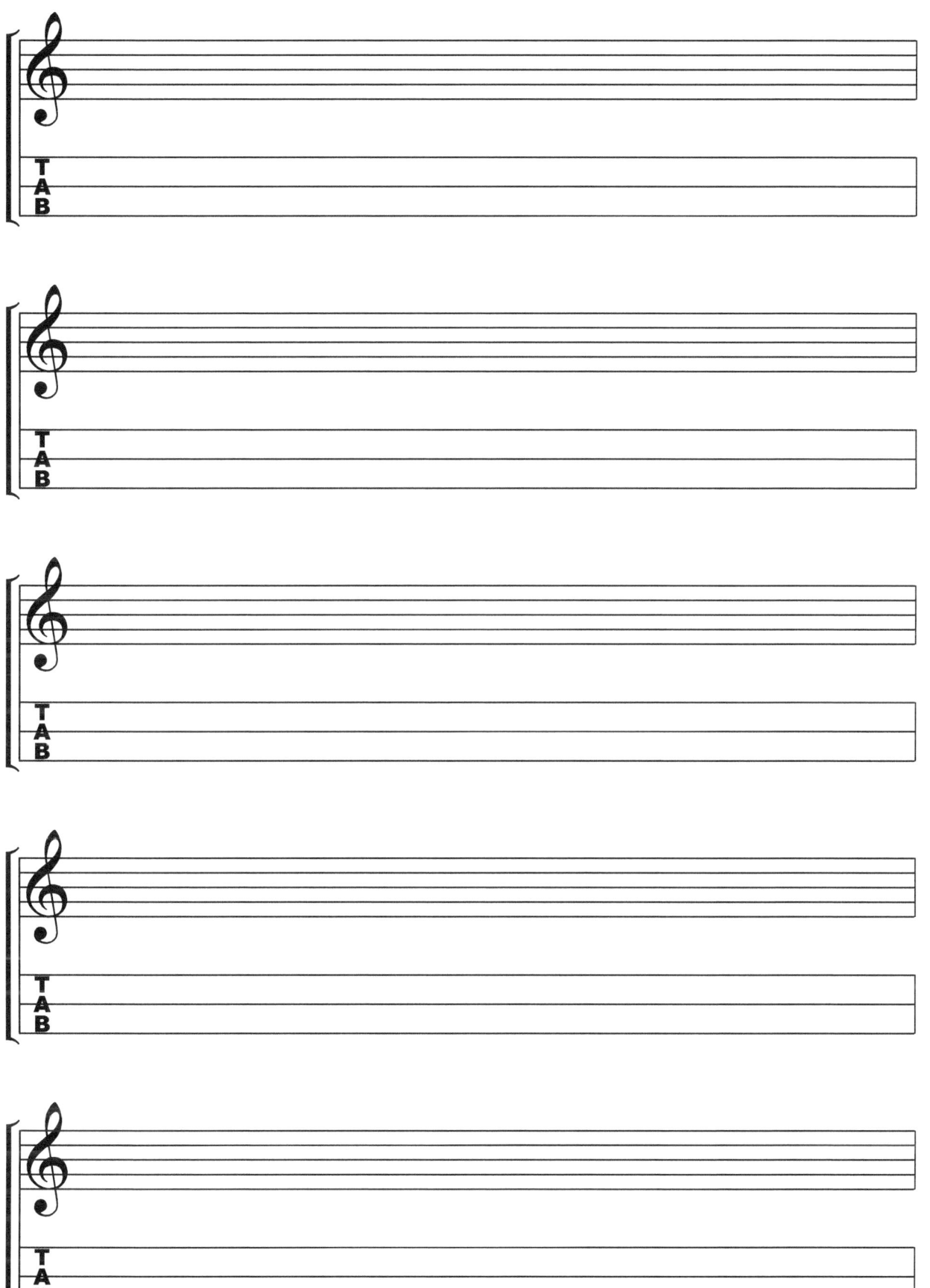

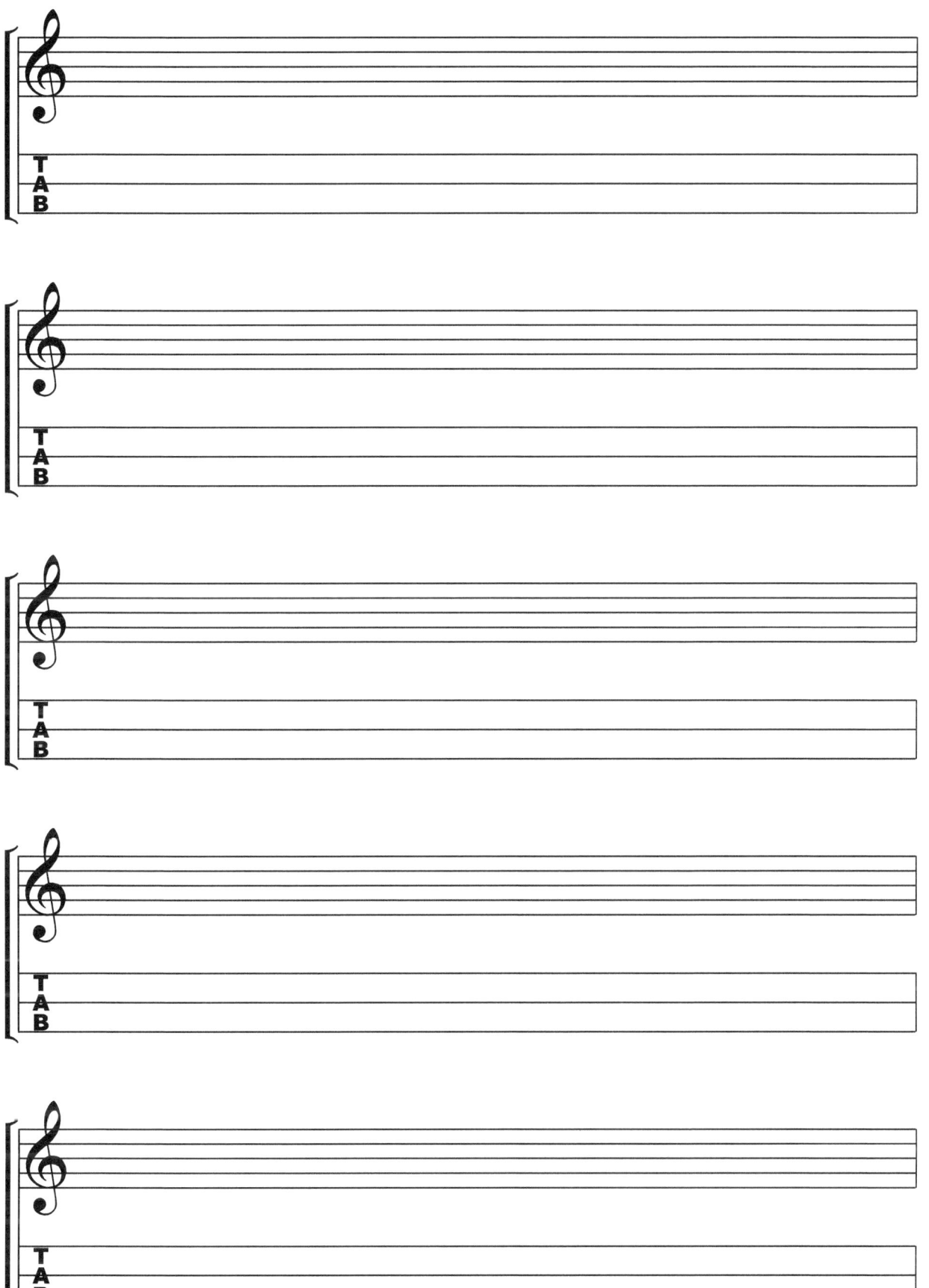

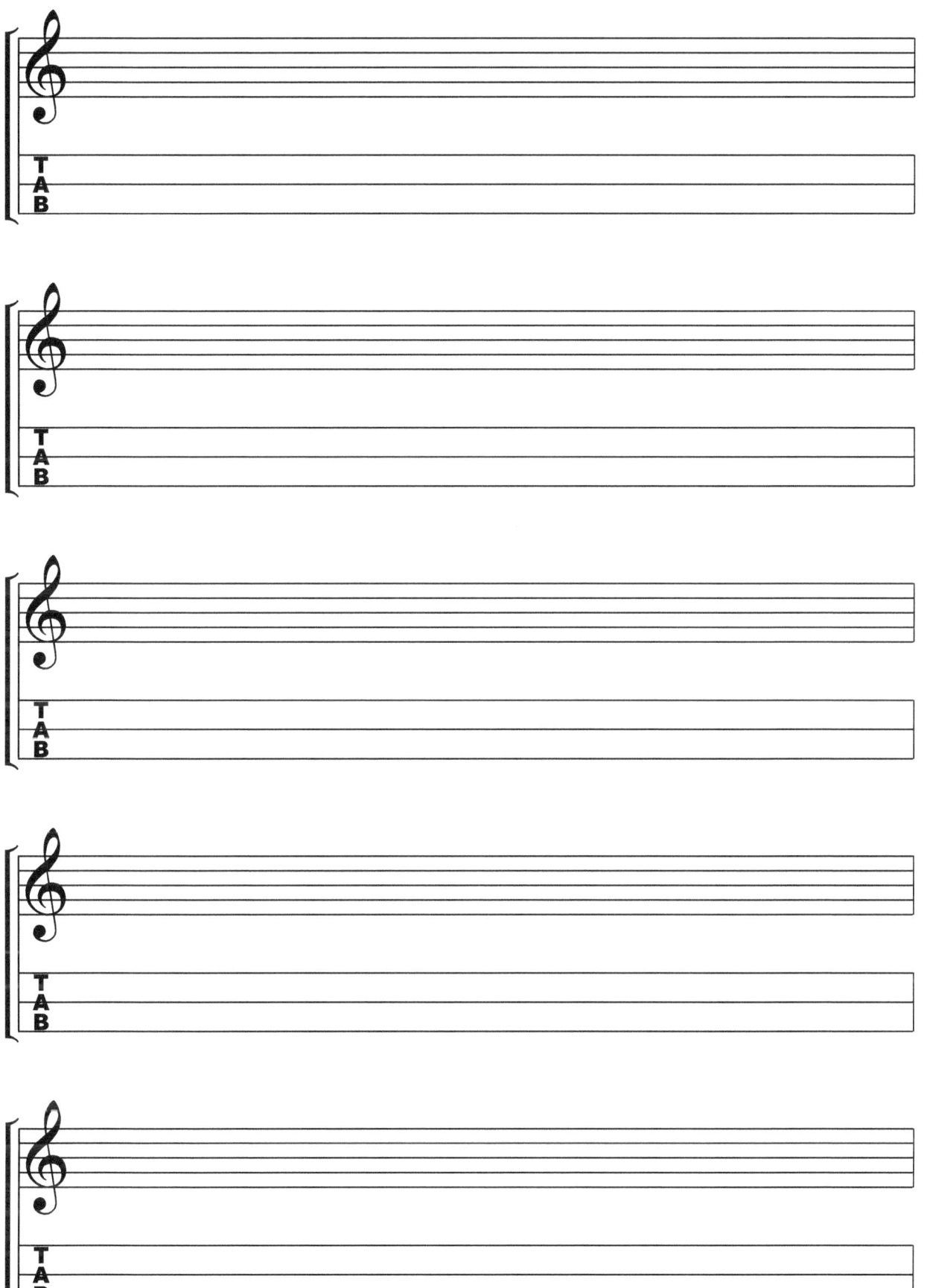

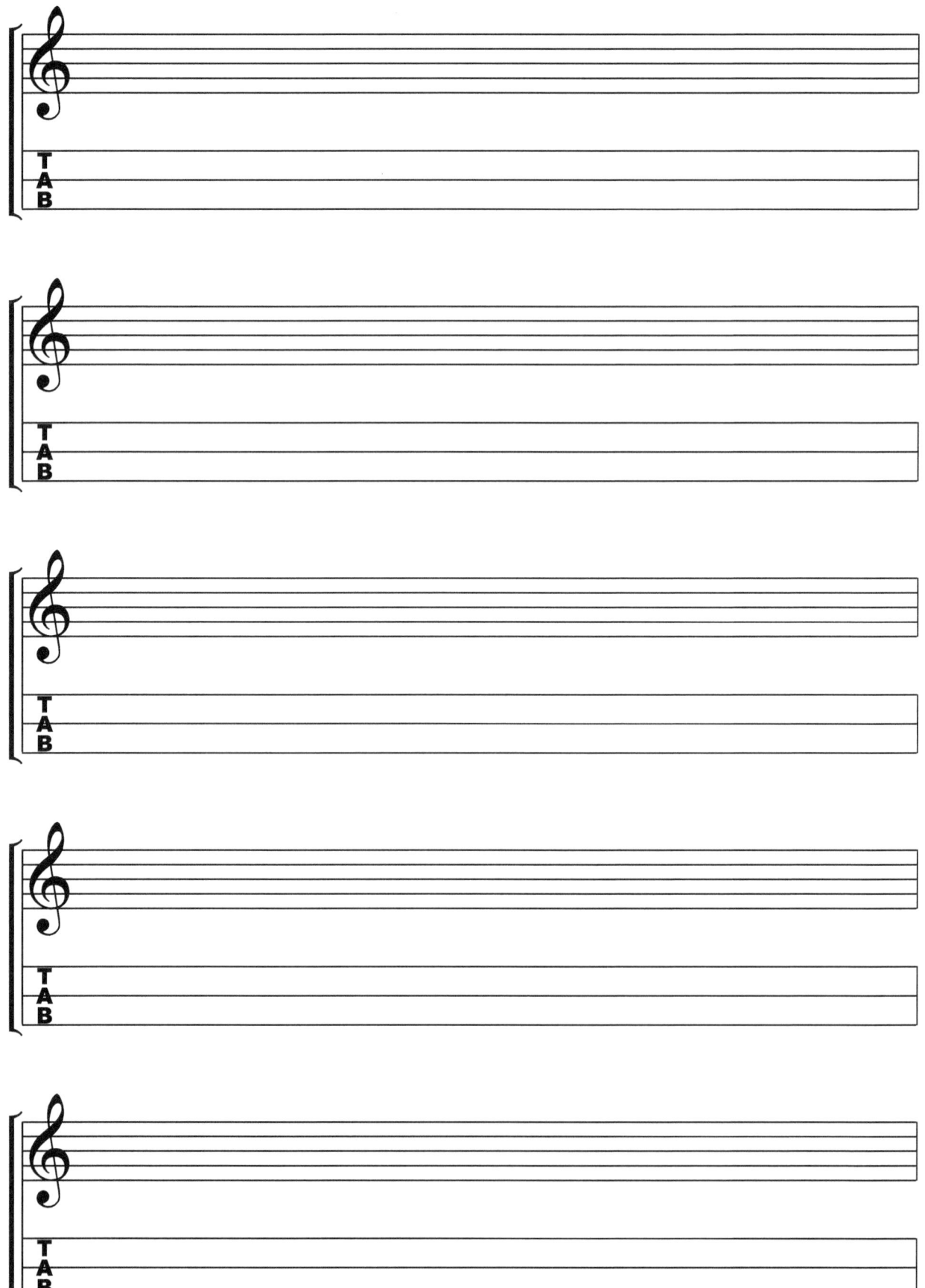

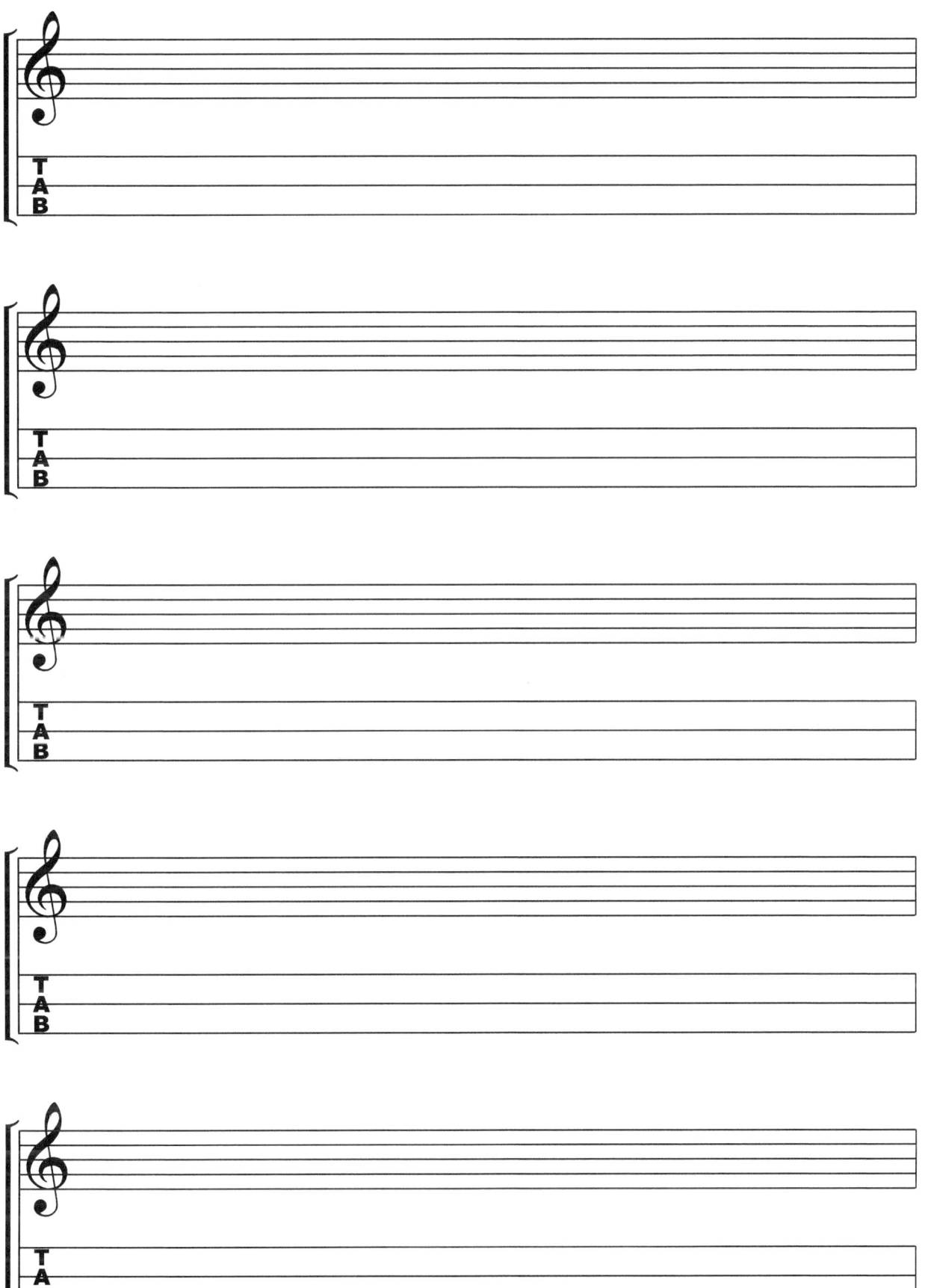

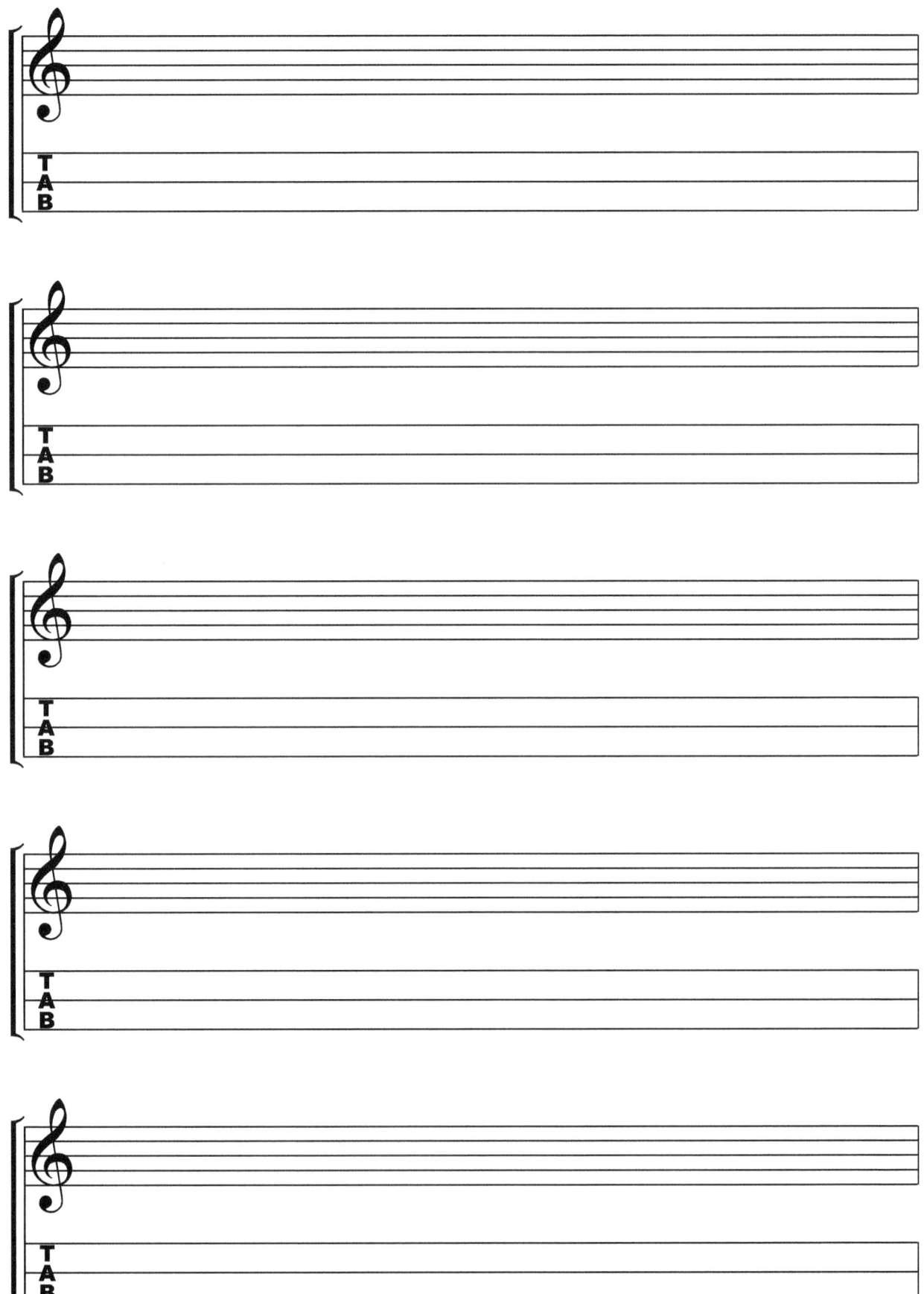

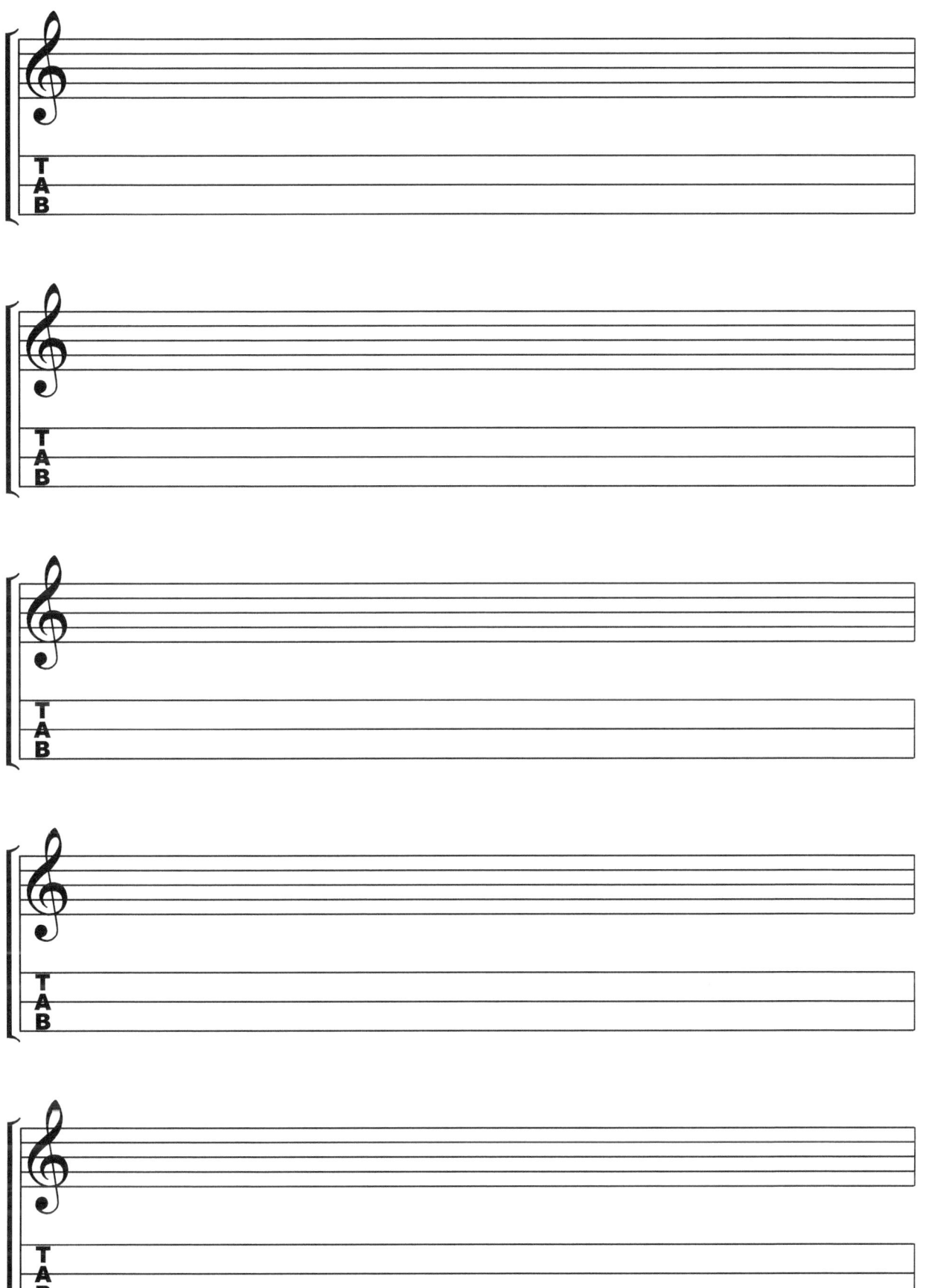

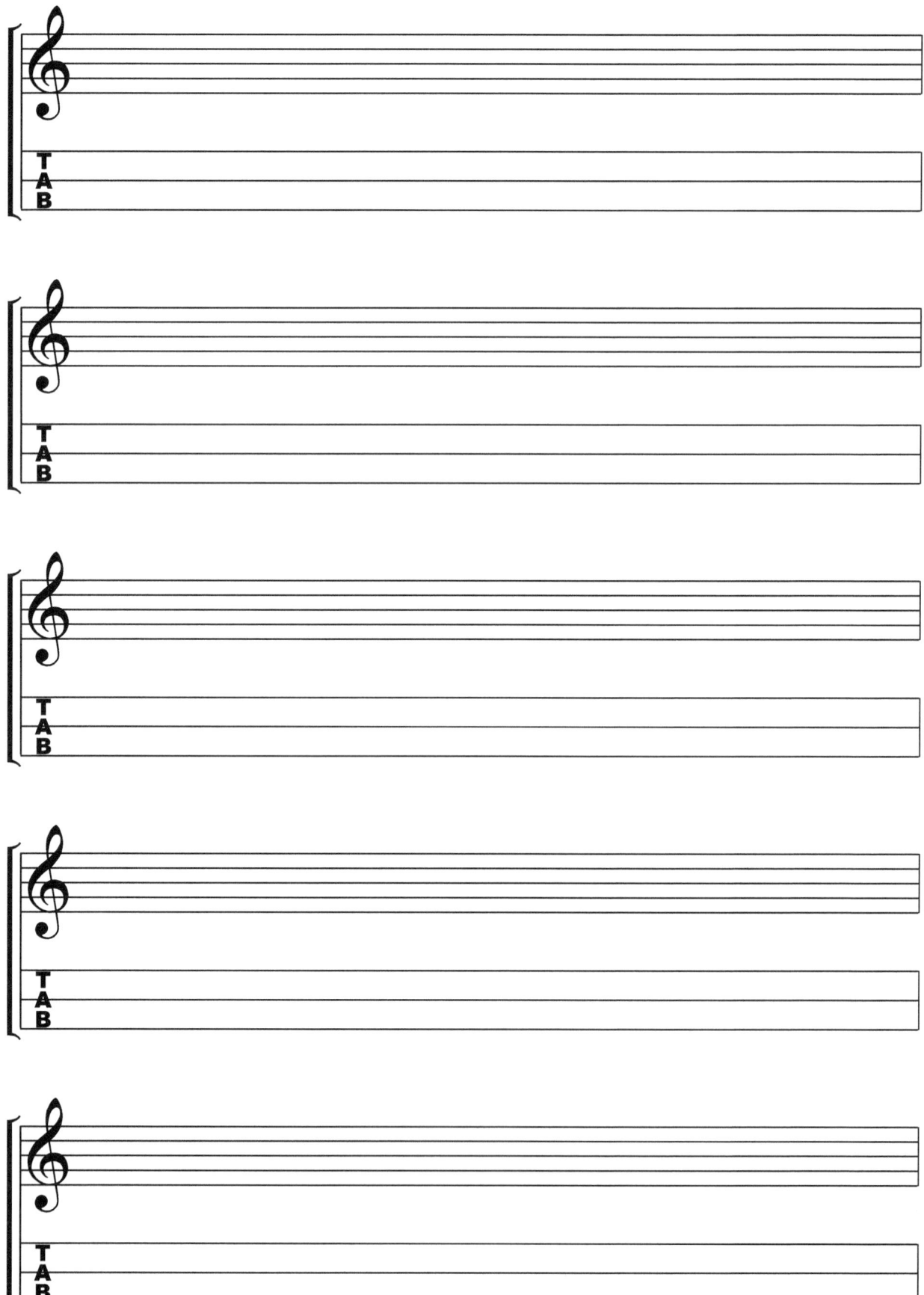

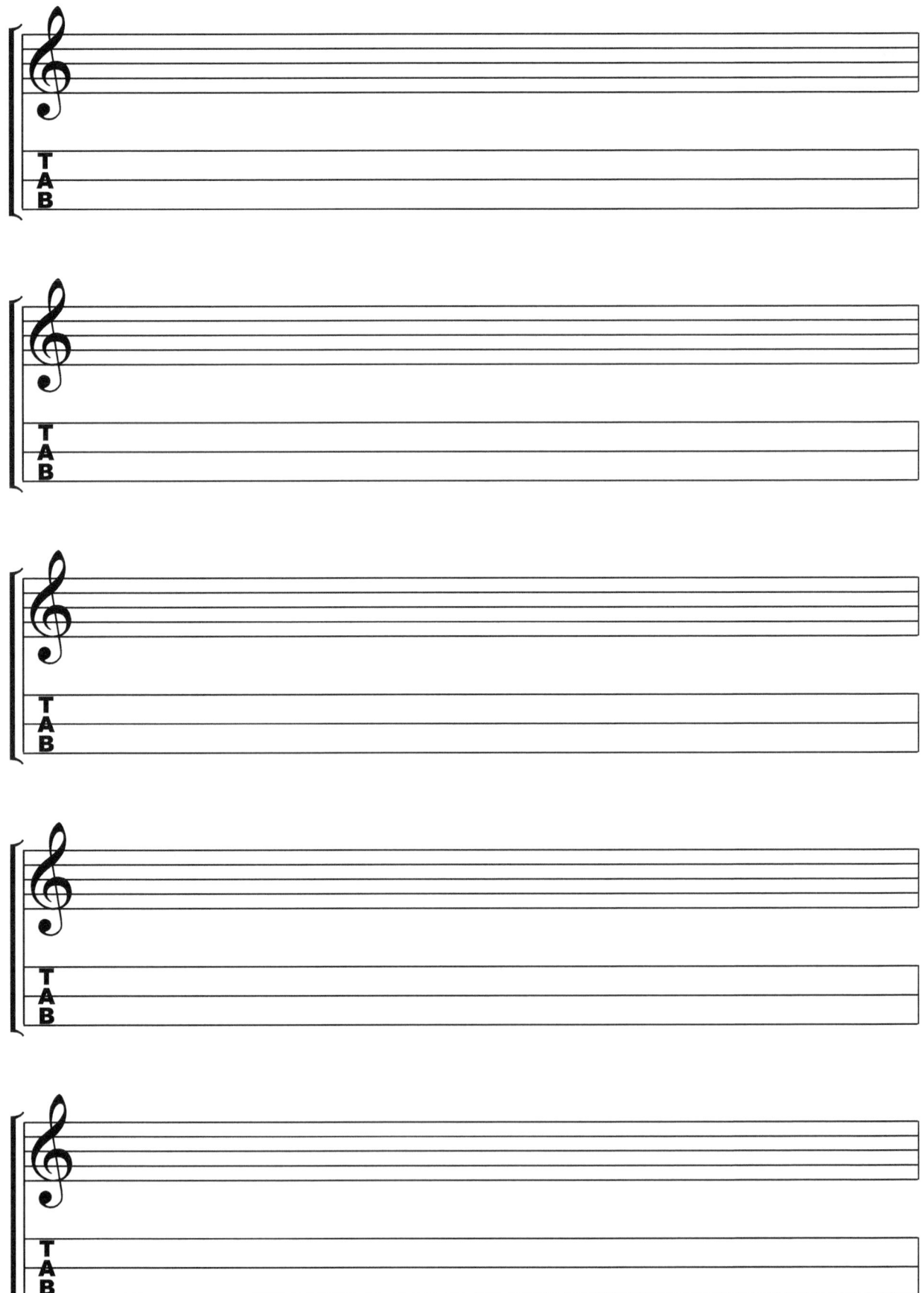

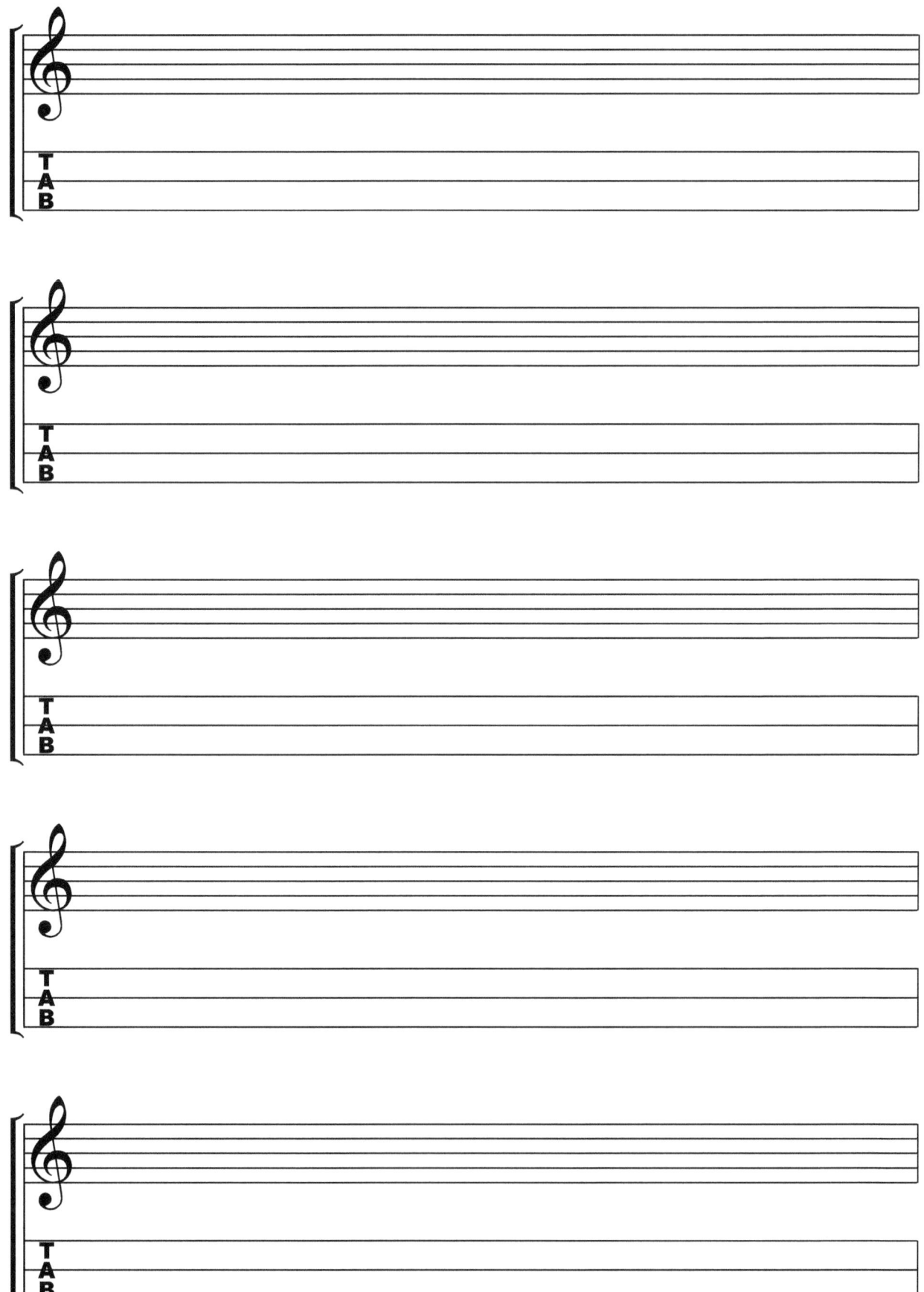

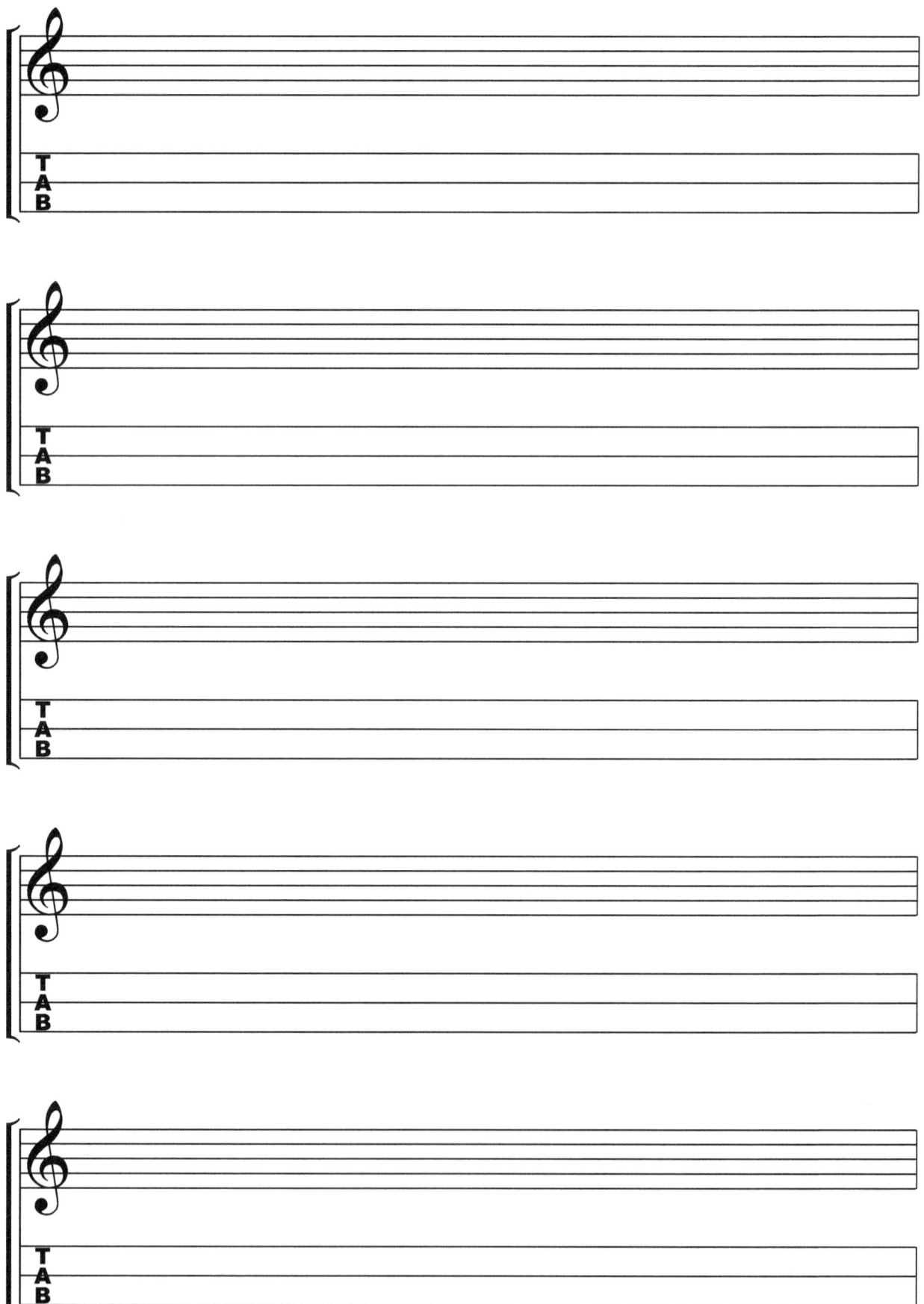

38

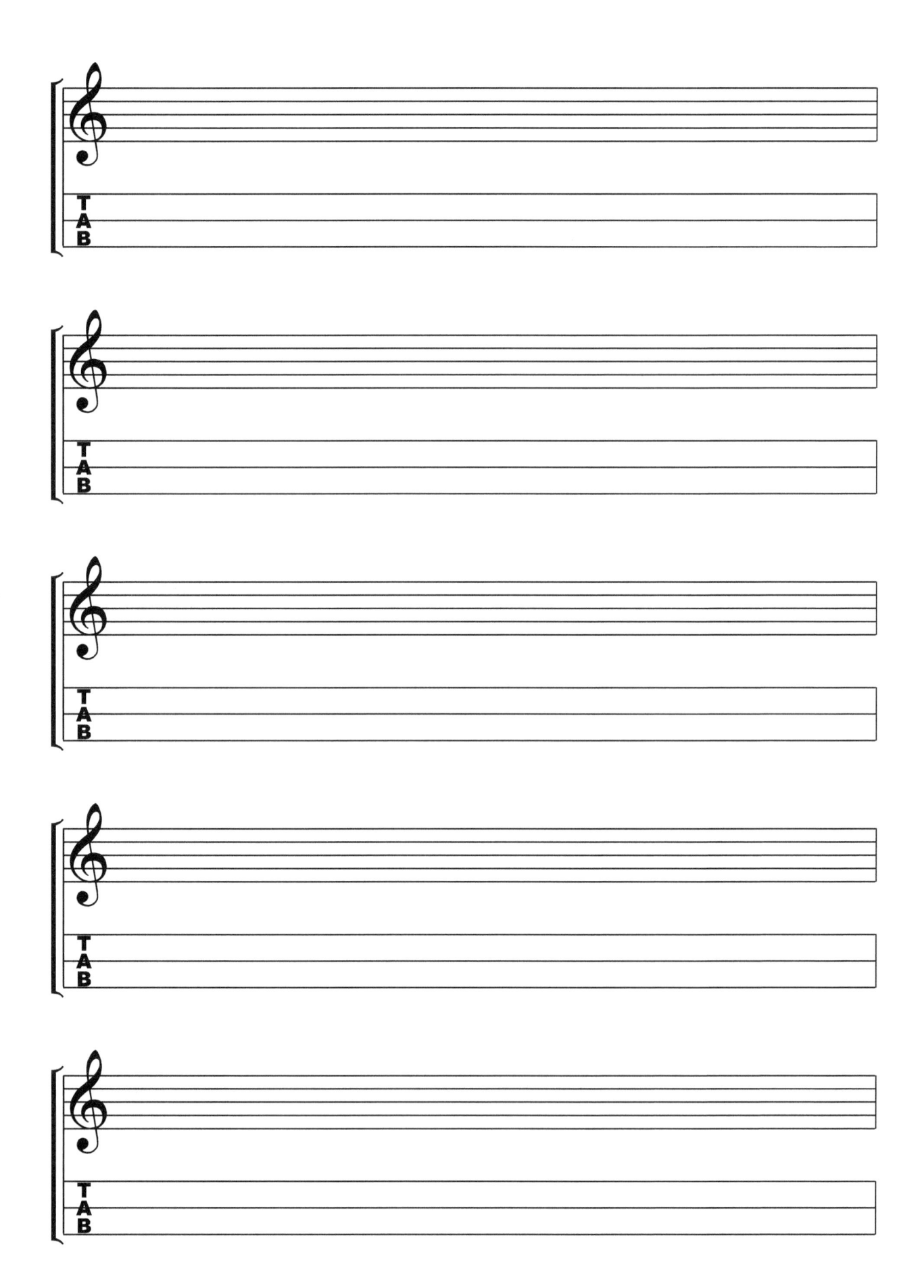

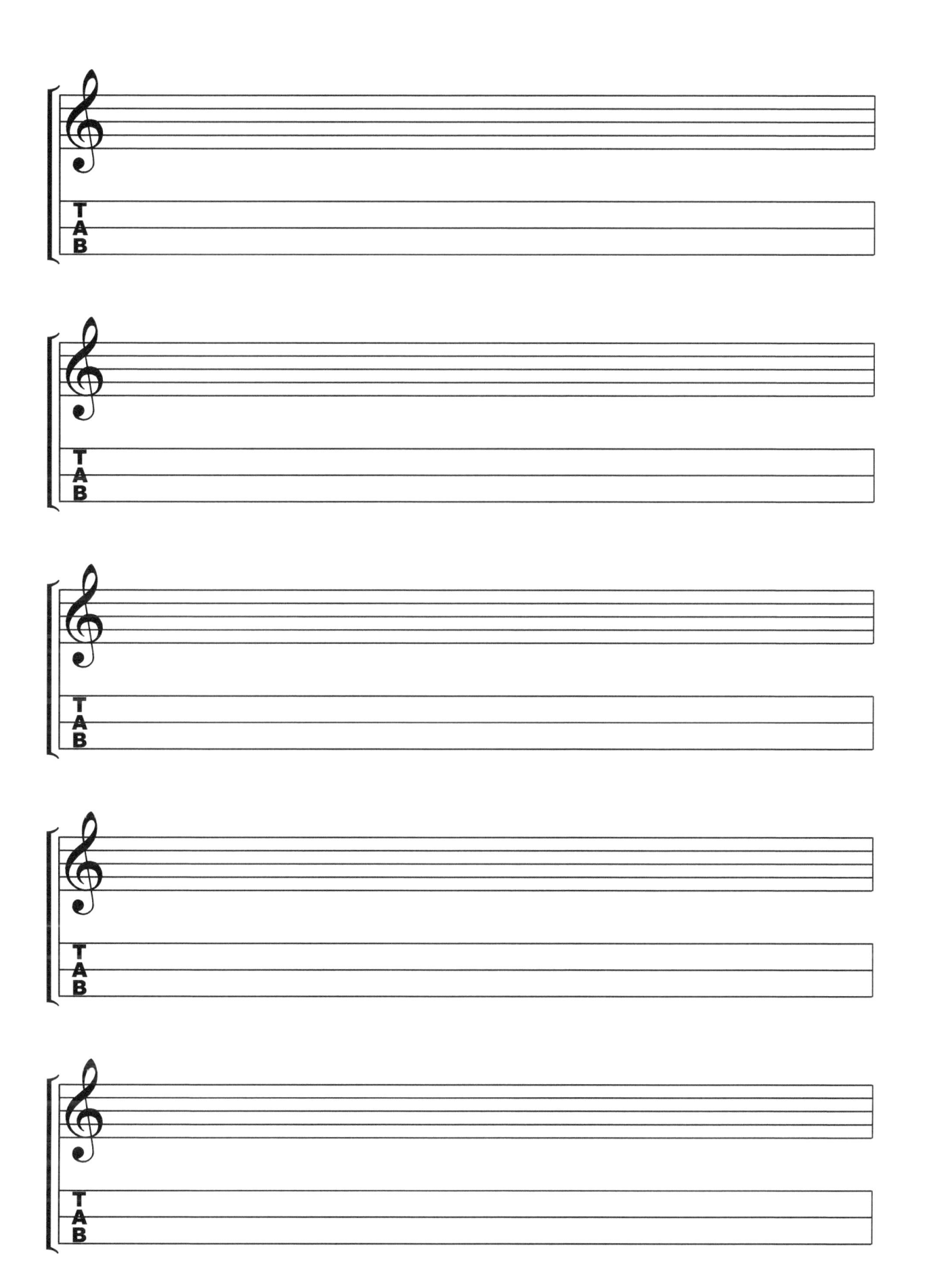

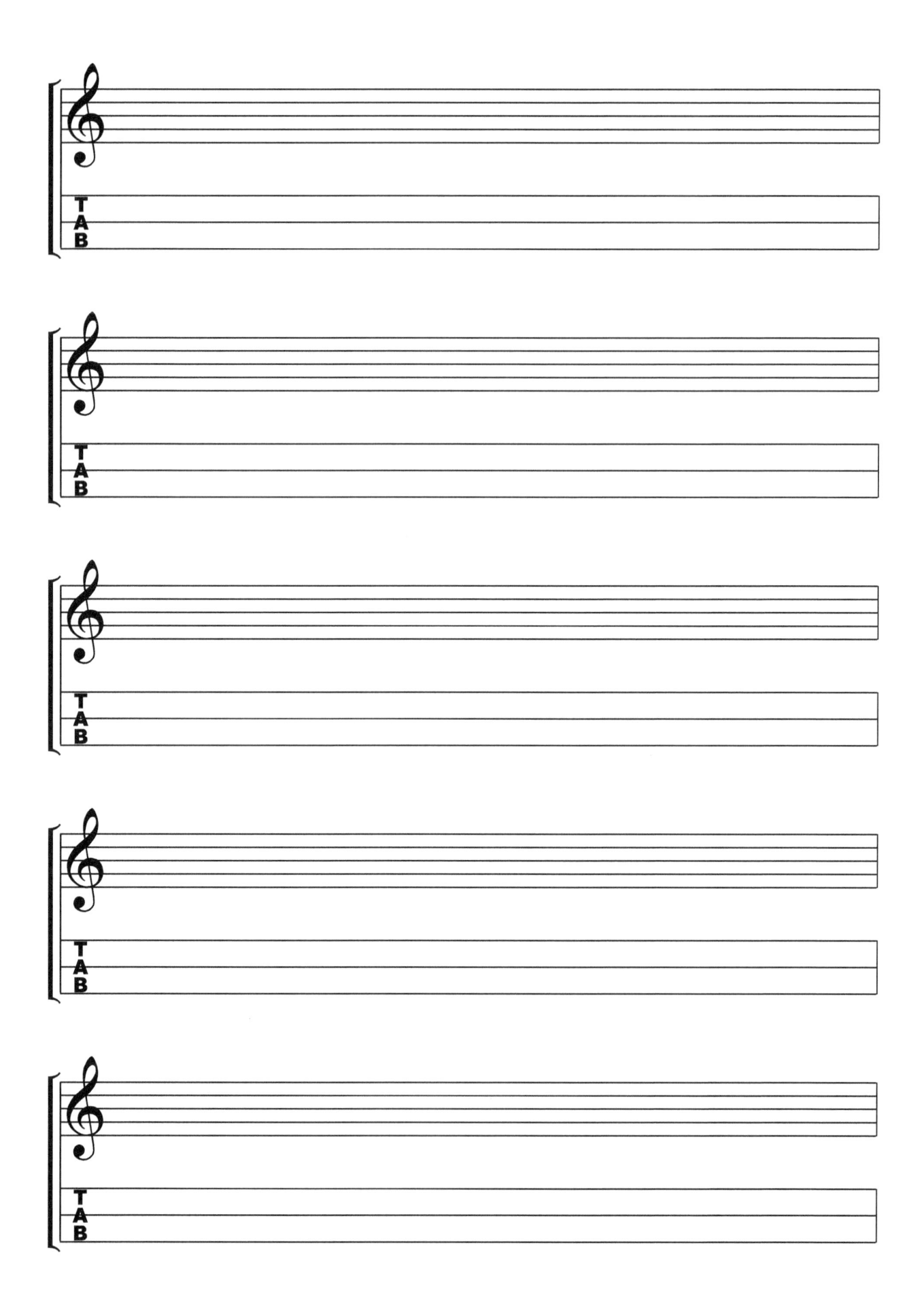

49

51

57

61

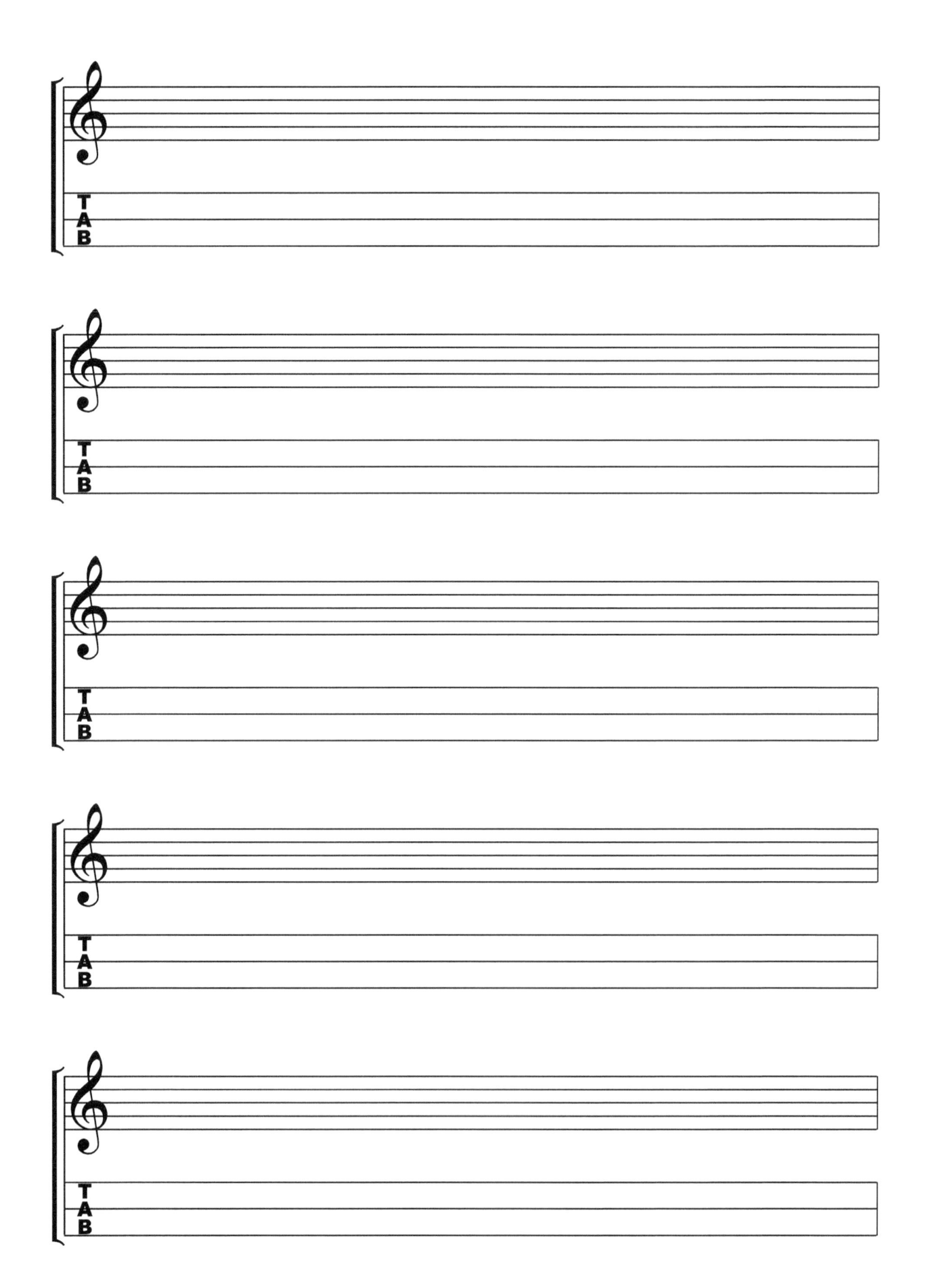

76

77

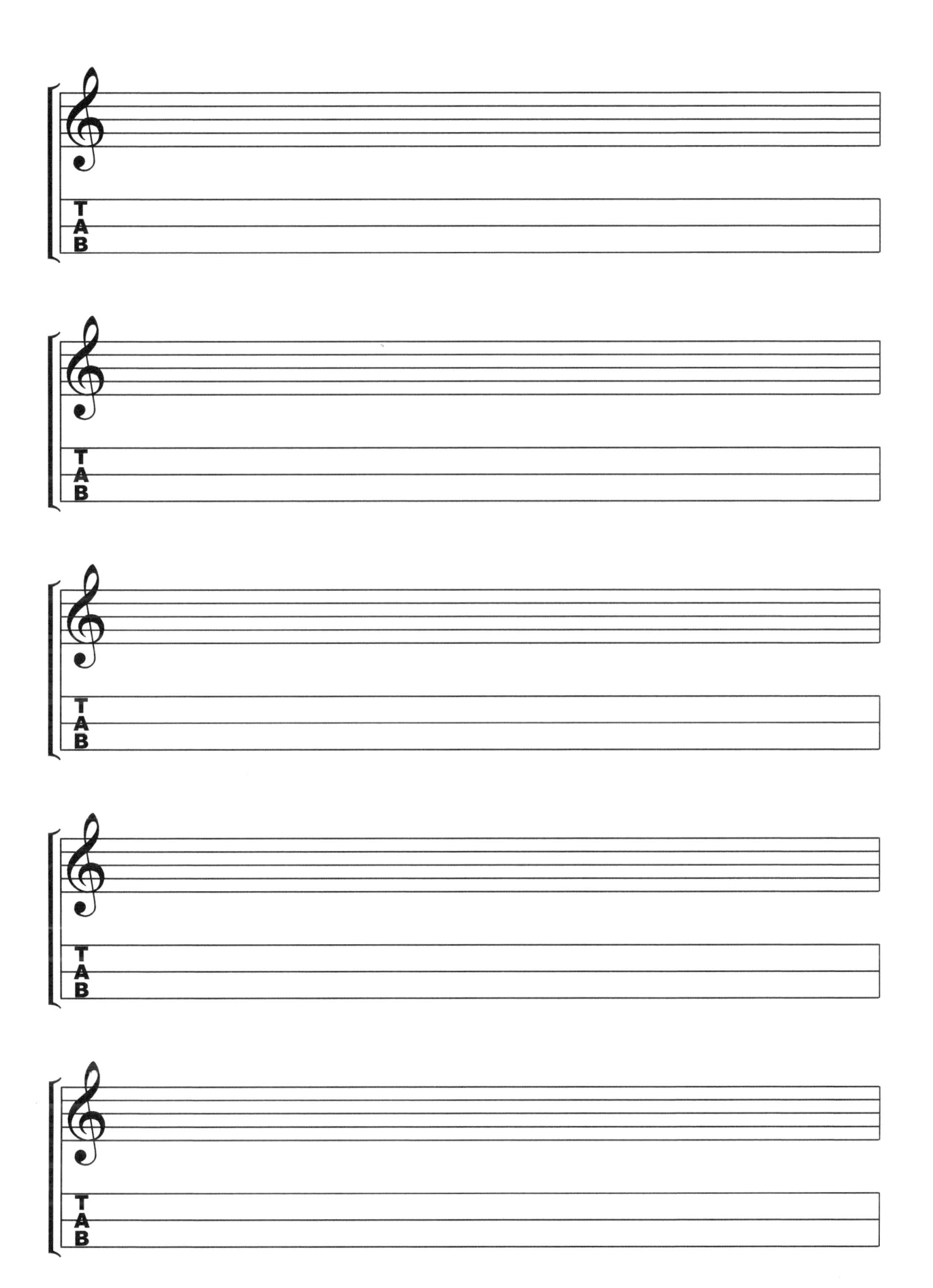

80

82

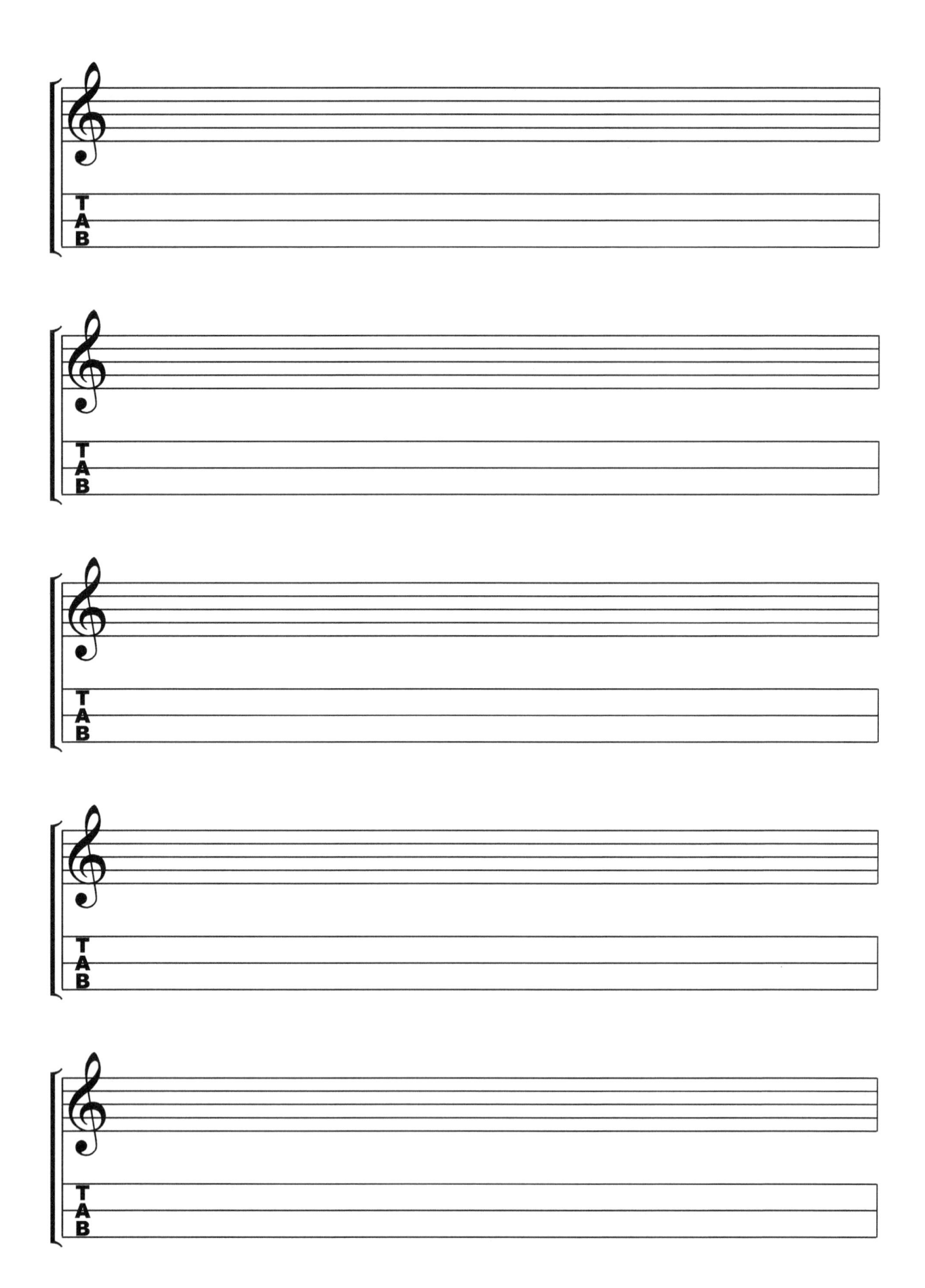

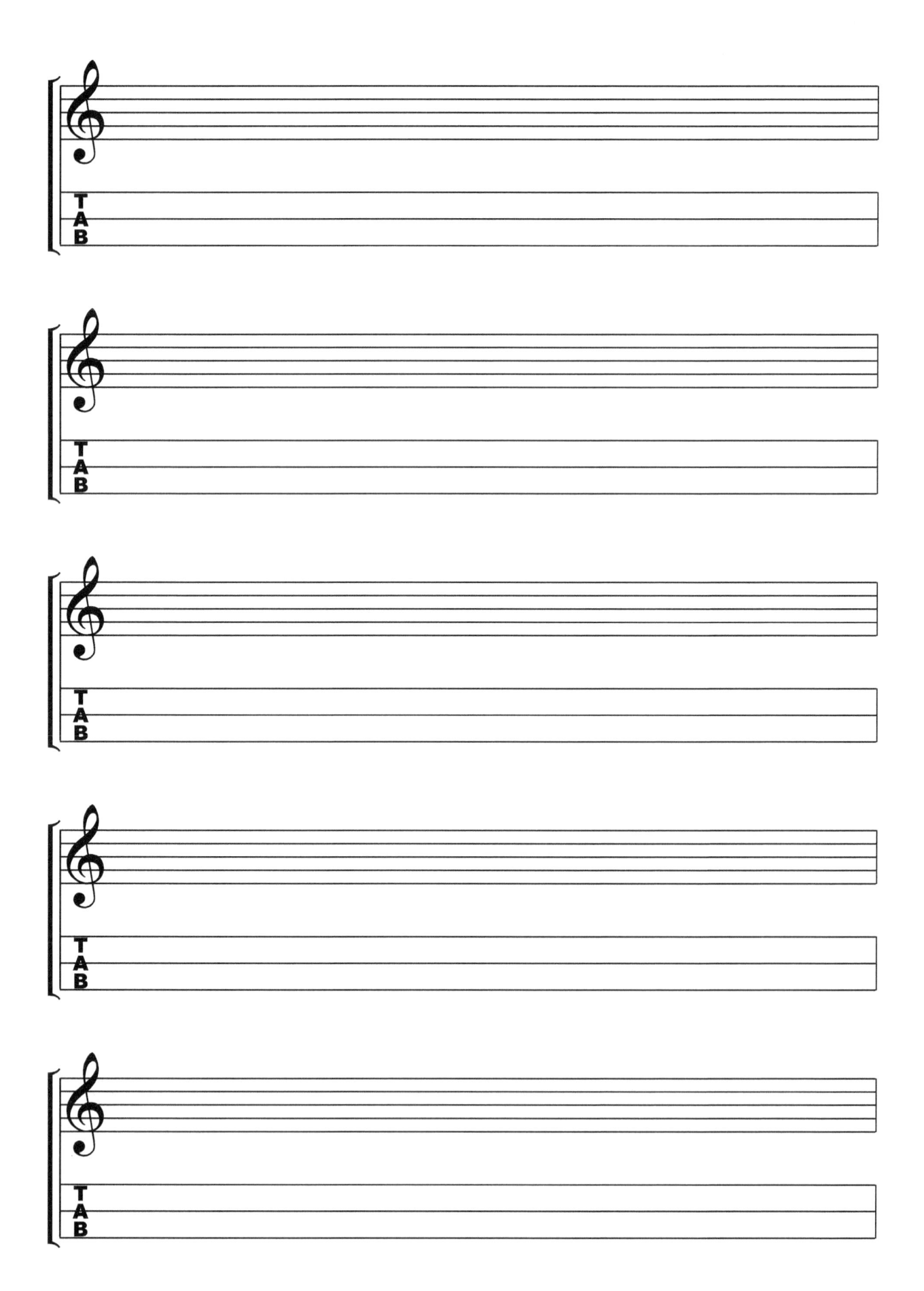

87

97

99

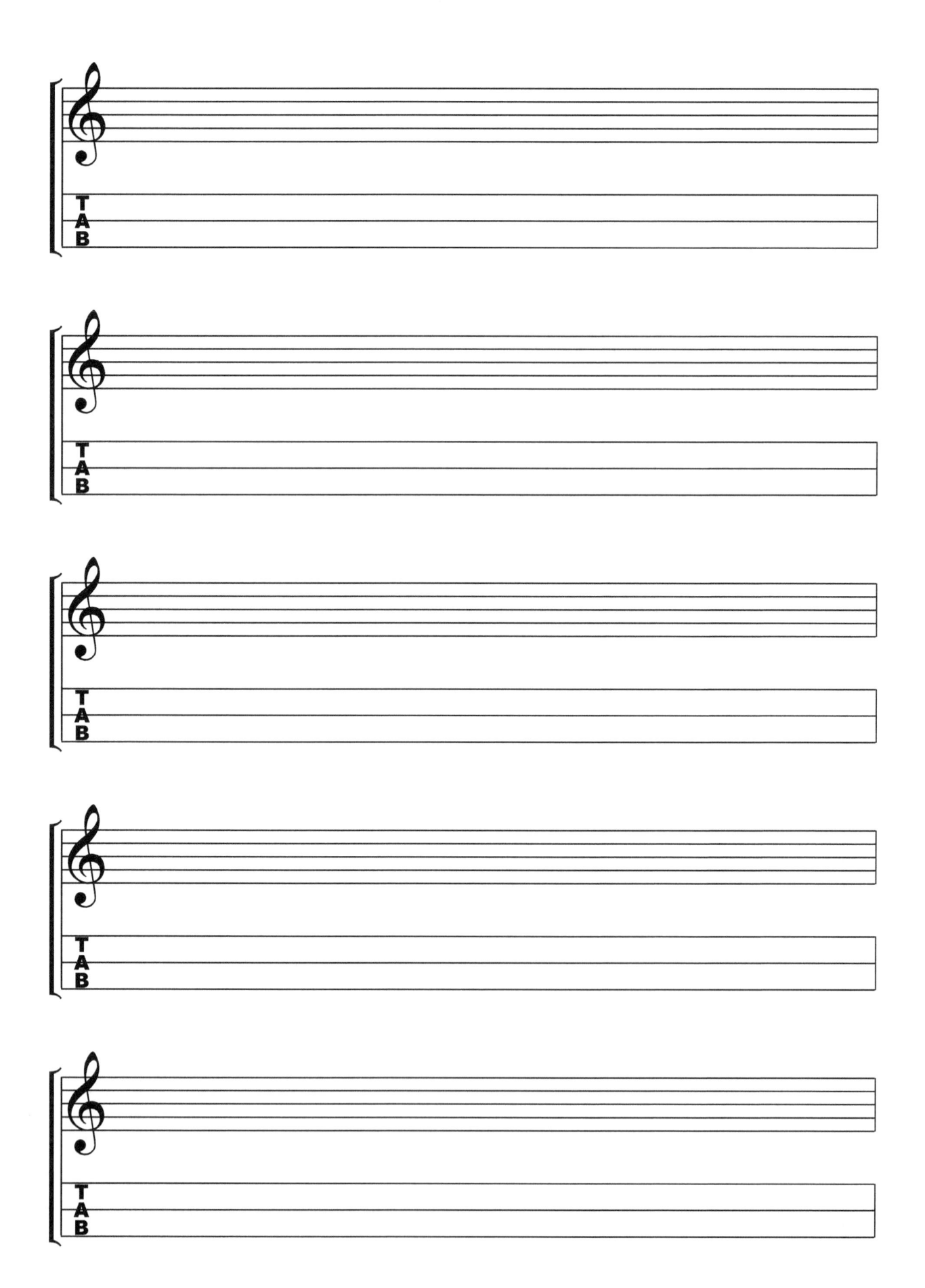

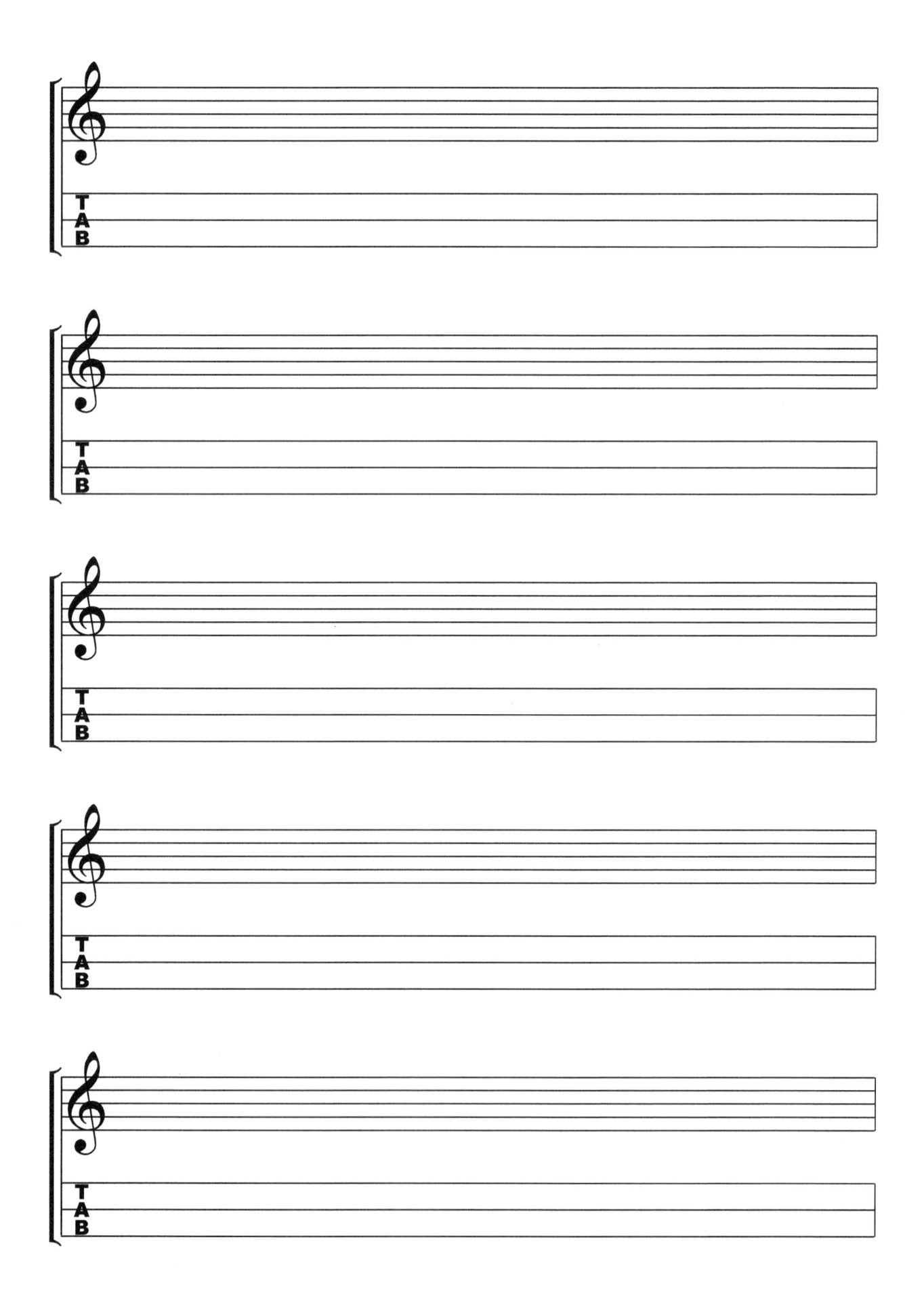

124

139

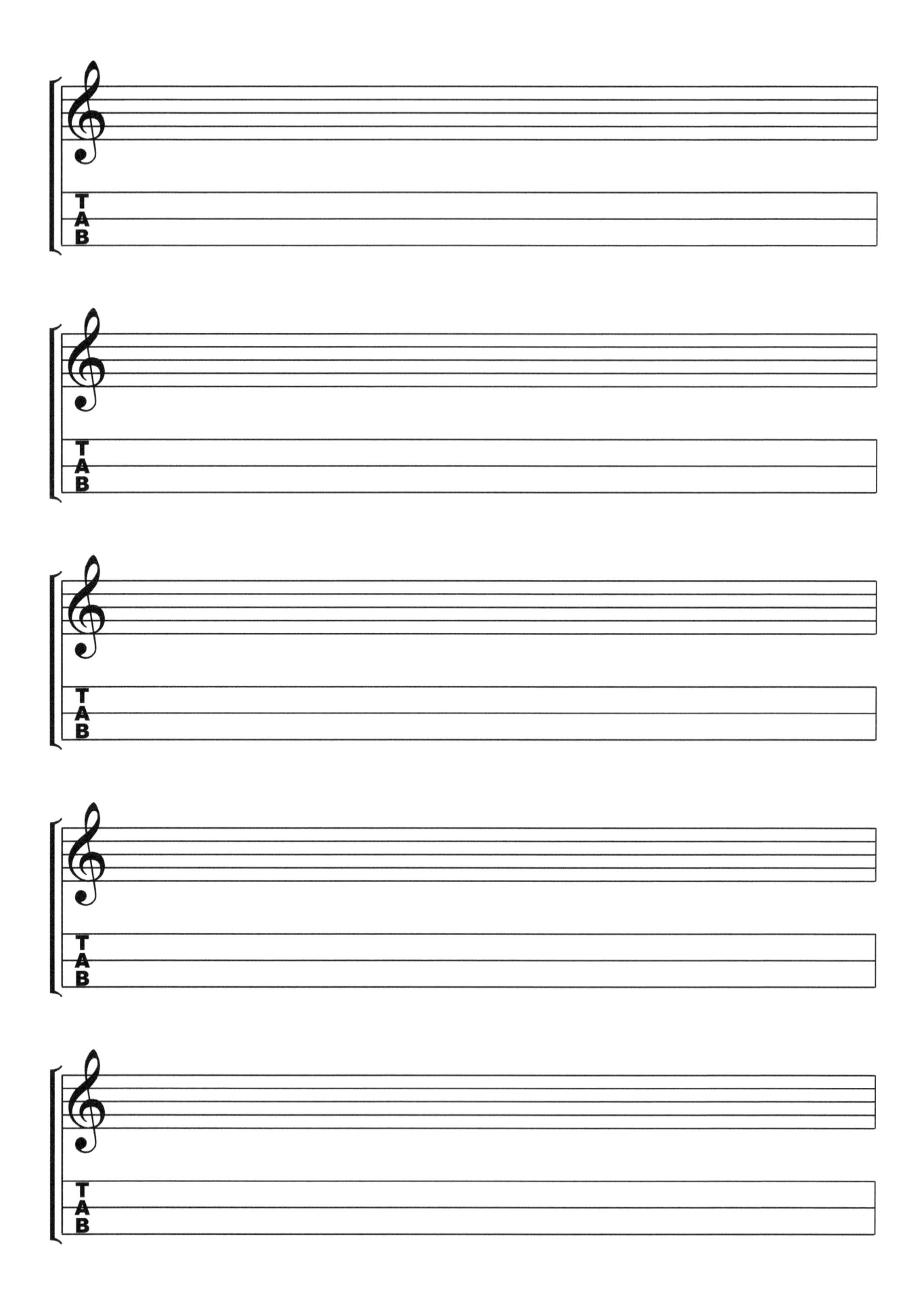

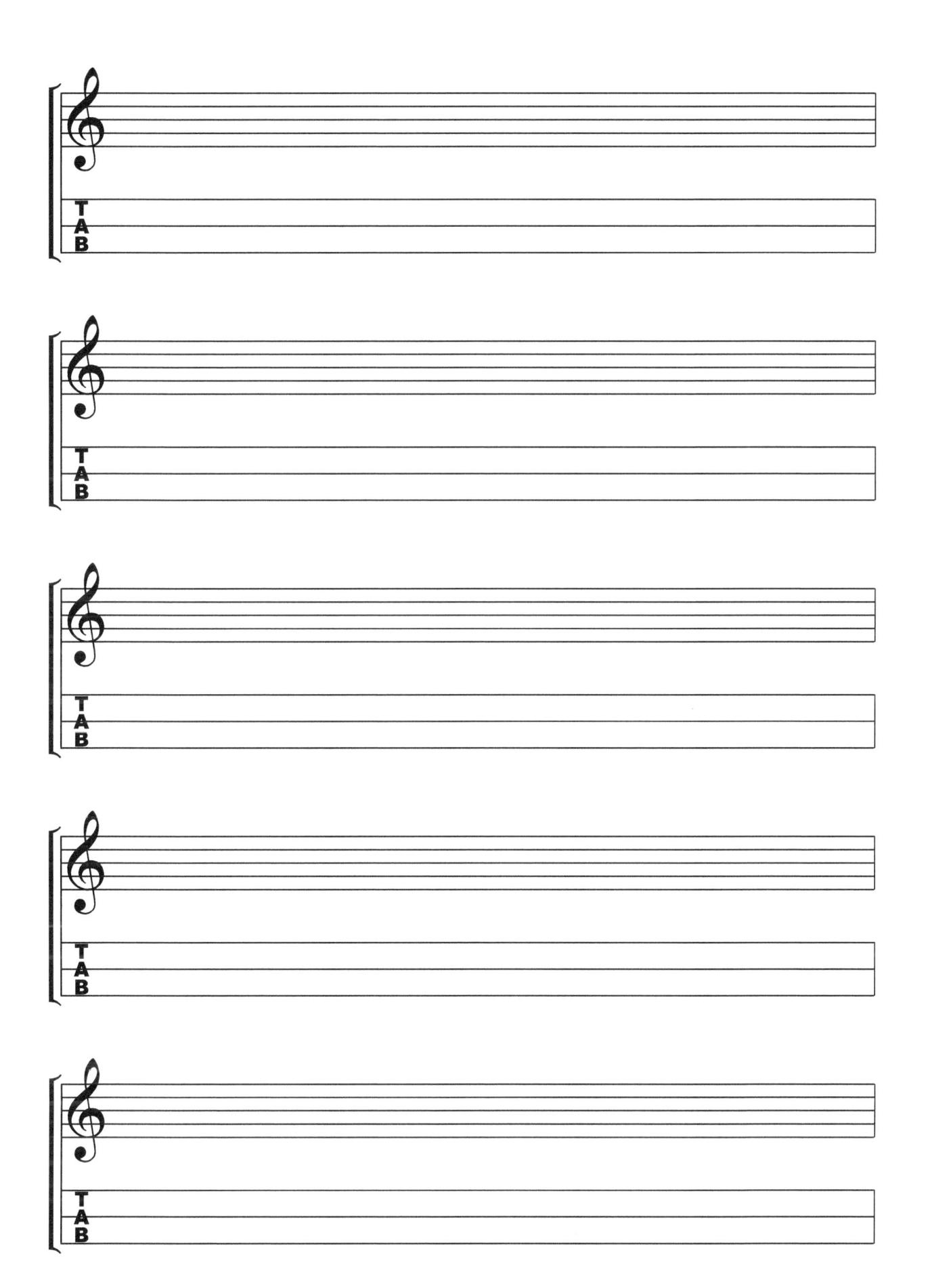

146

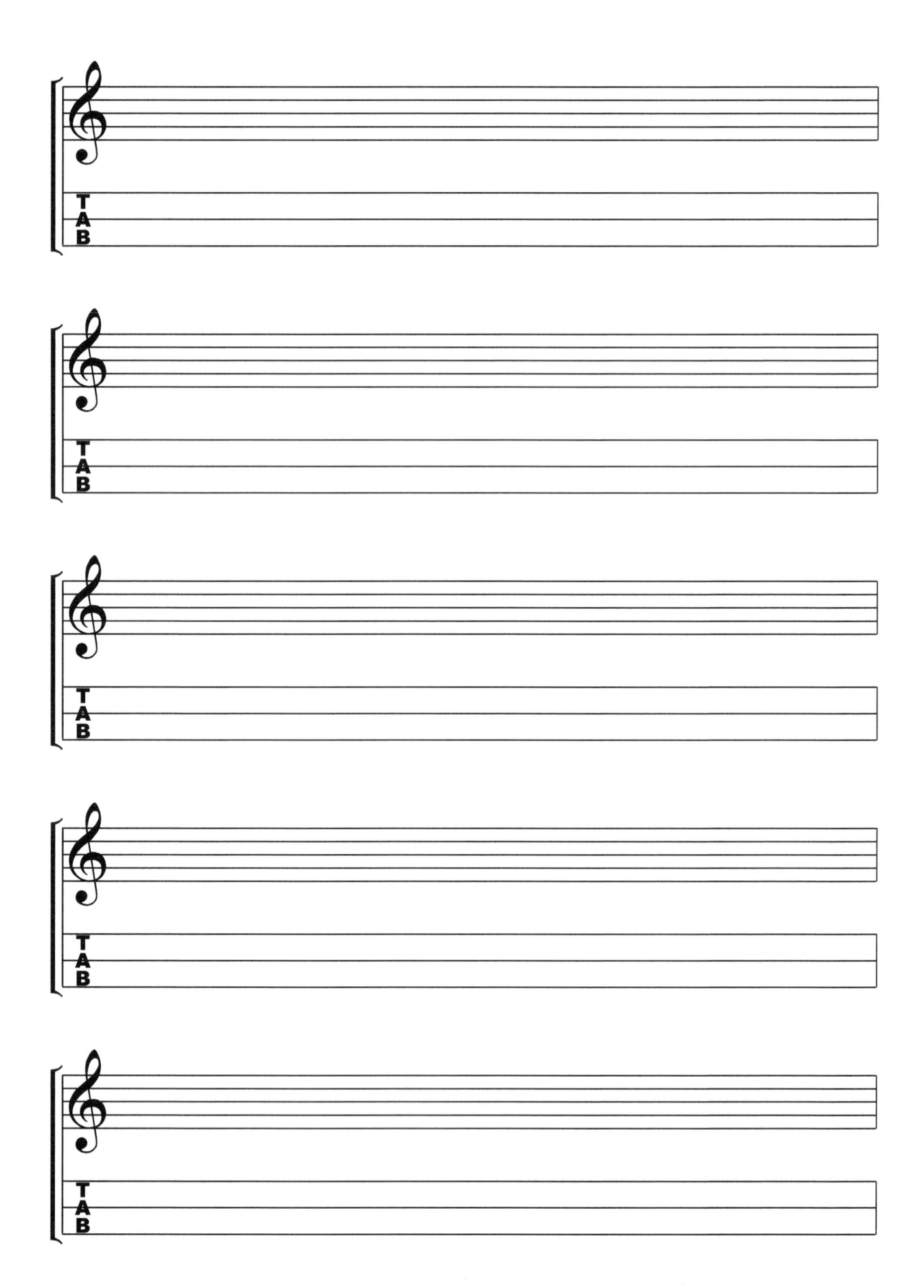

148

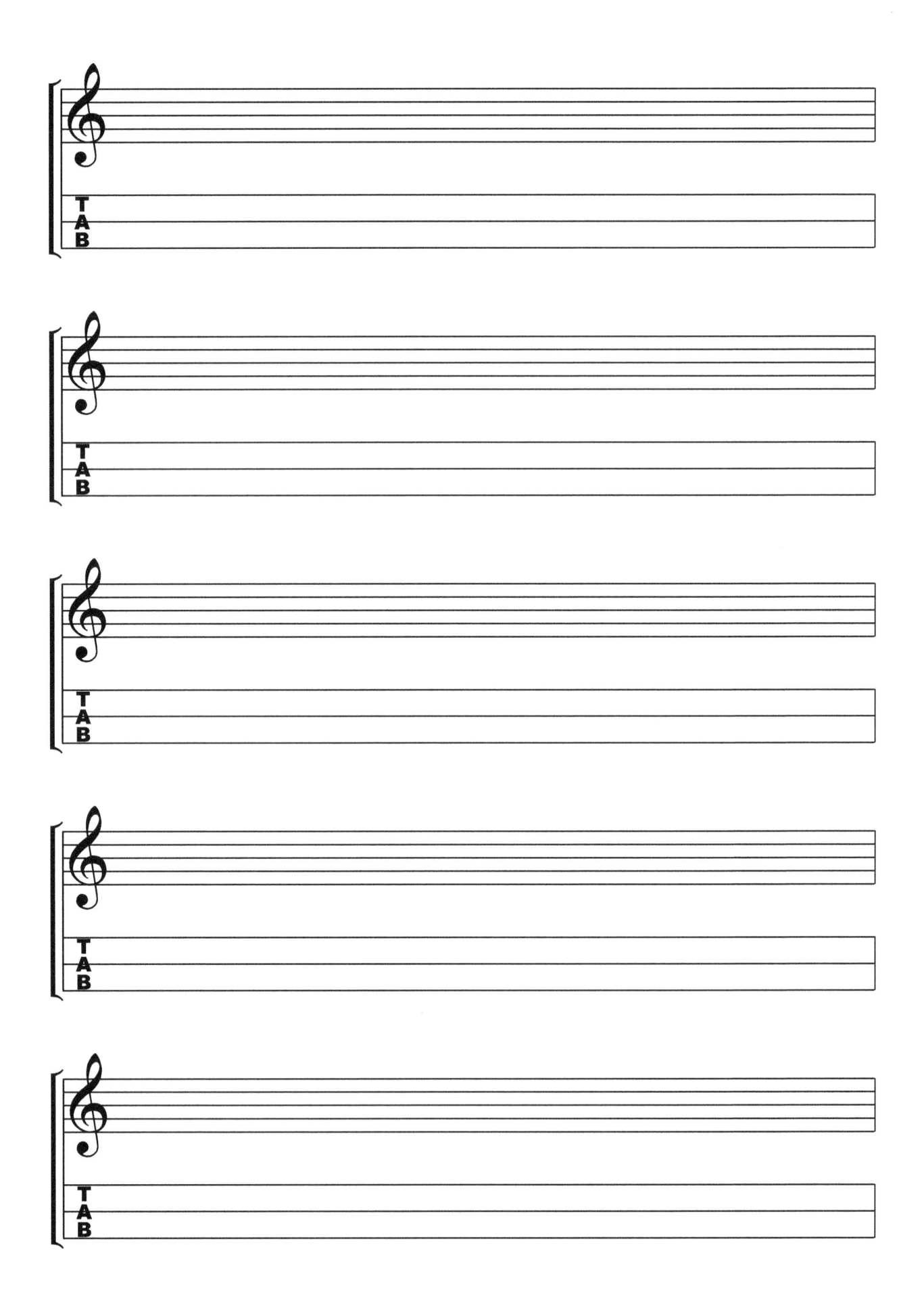

167

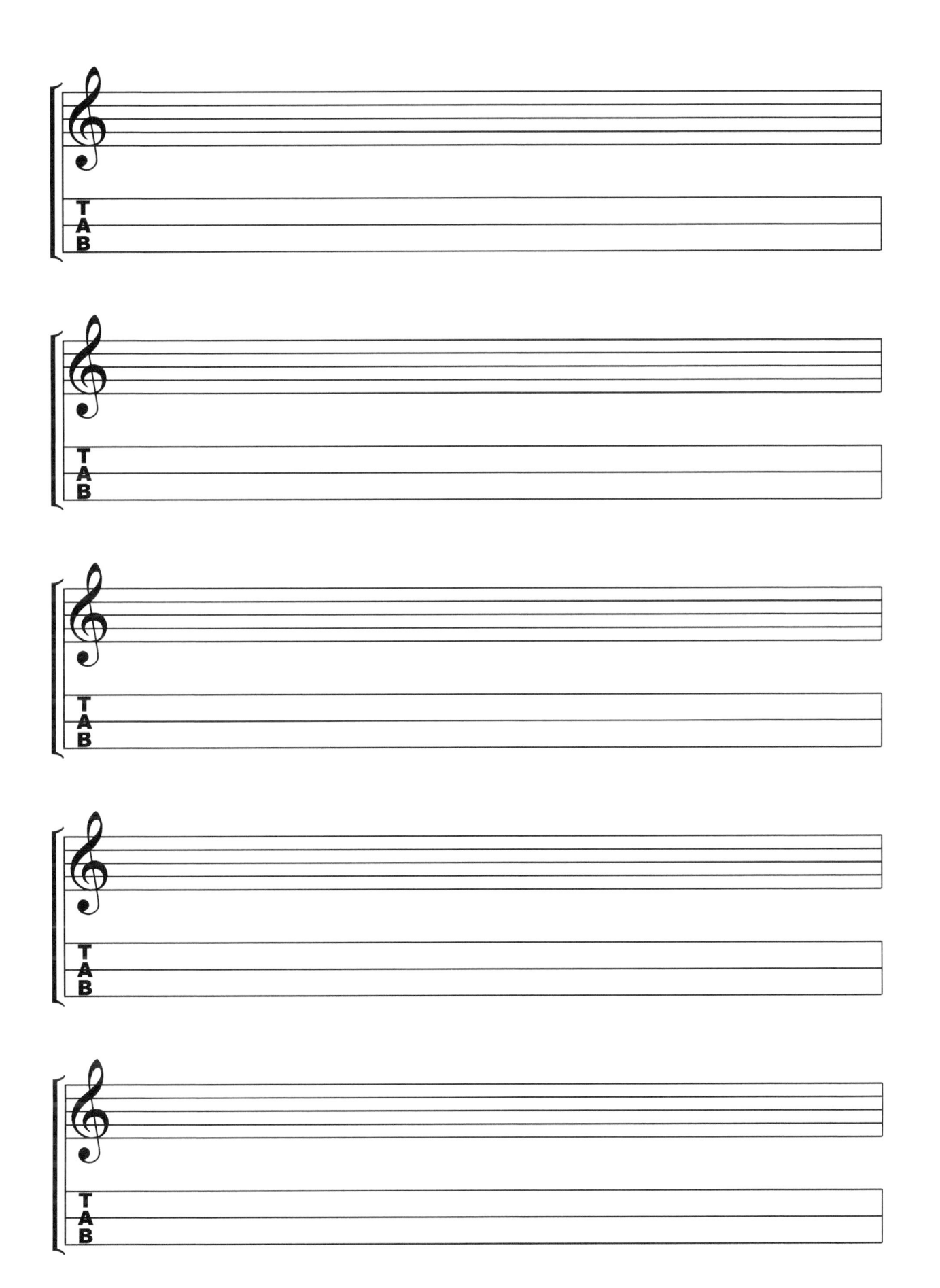

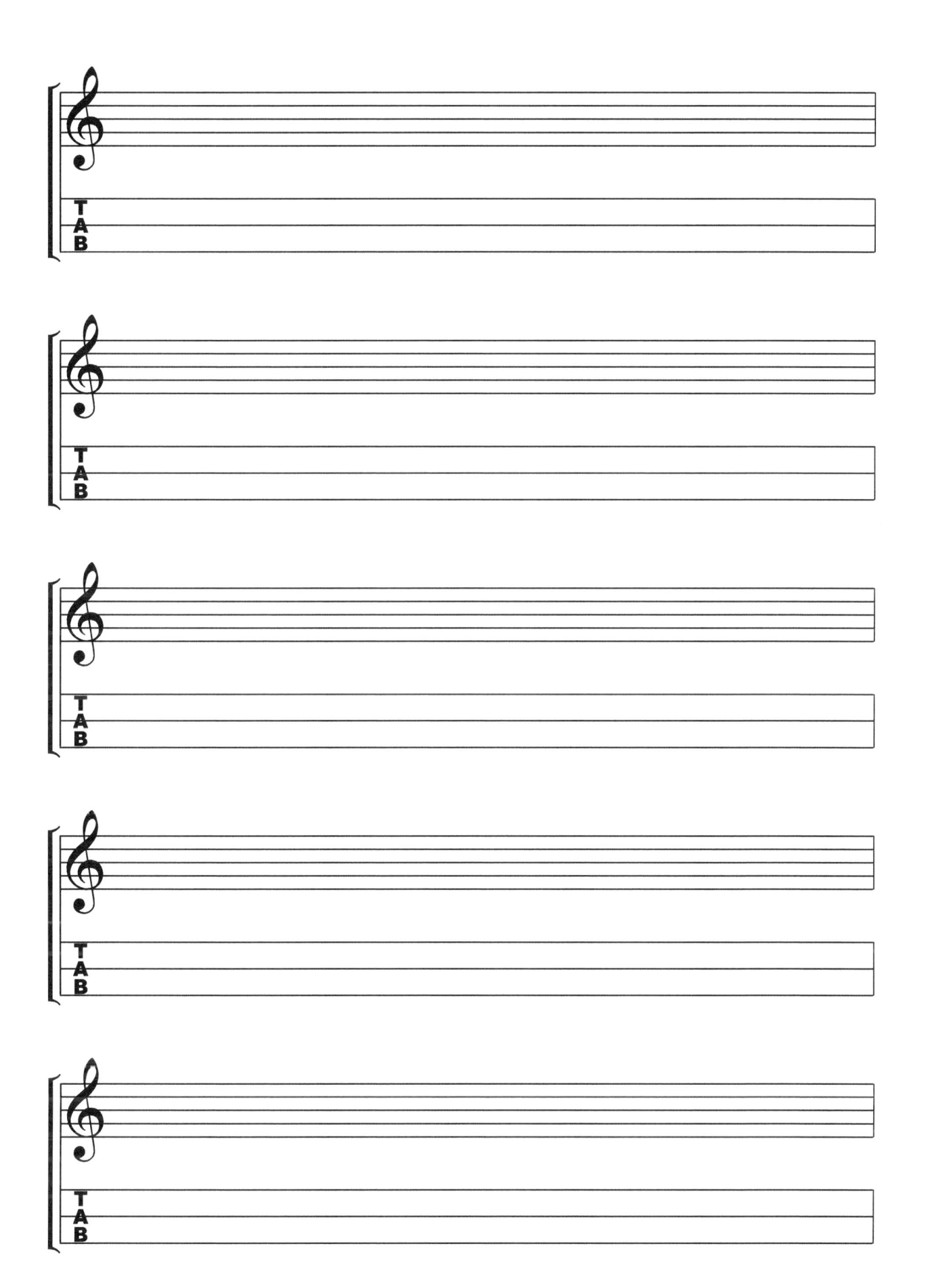

175

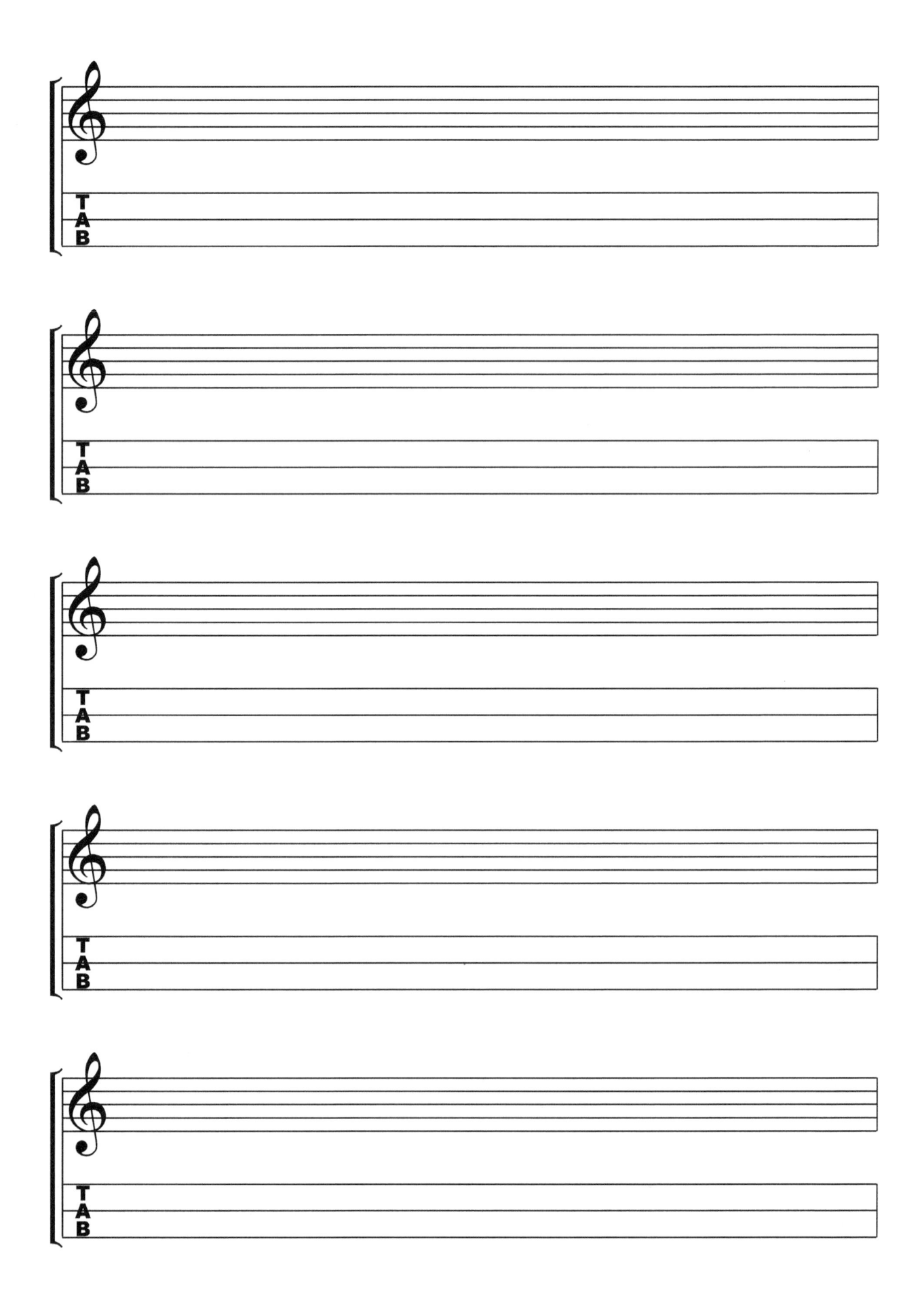

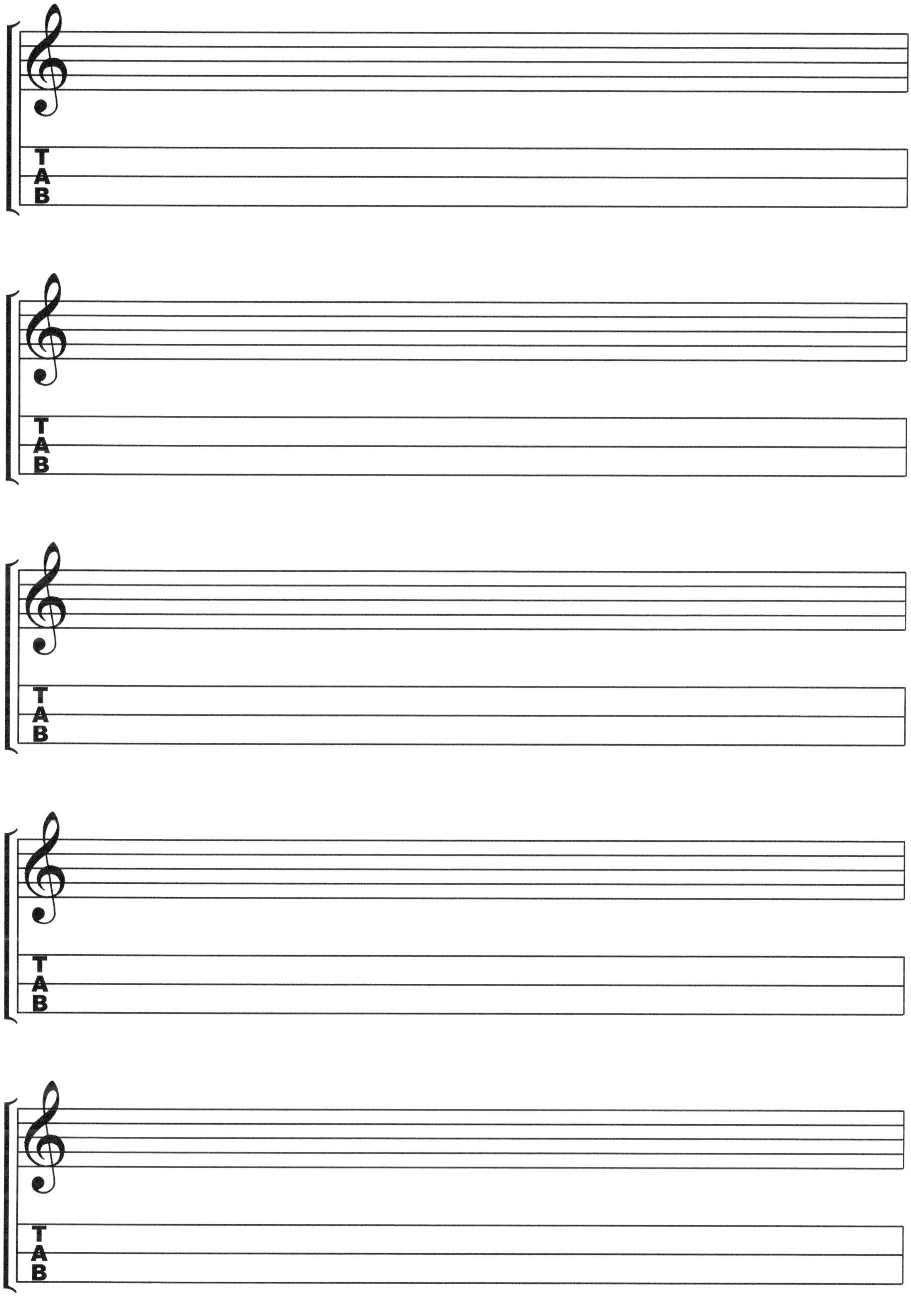

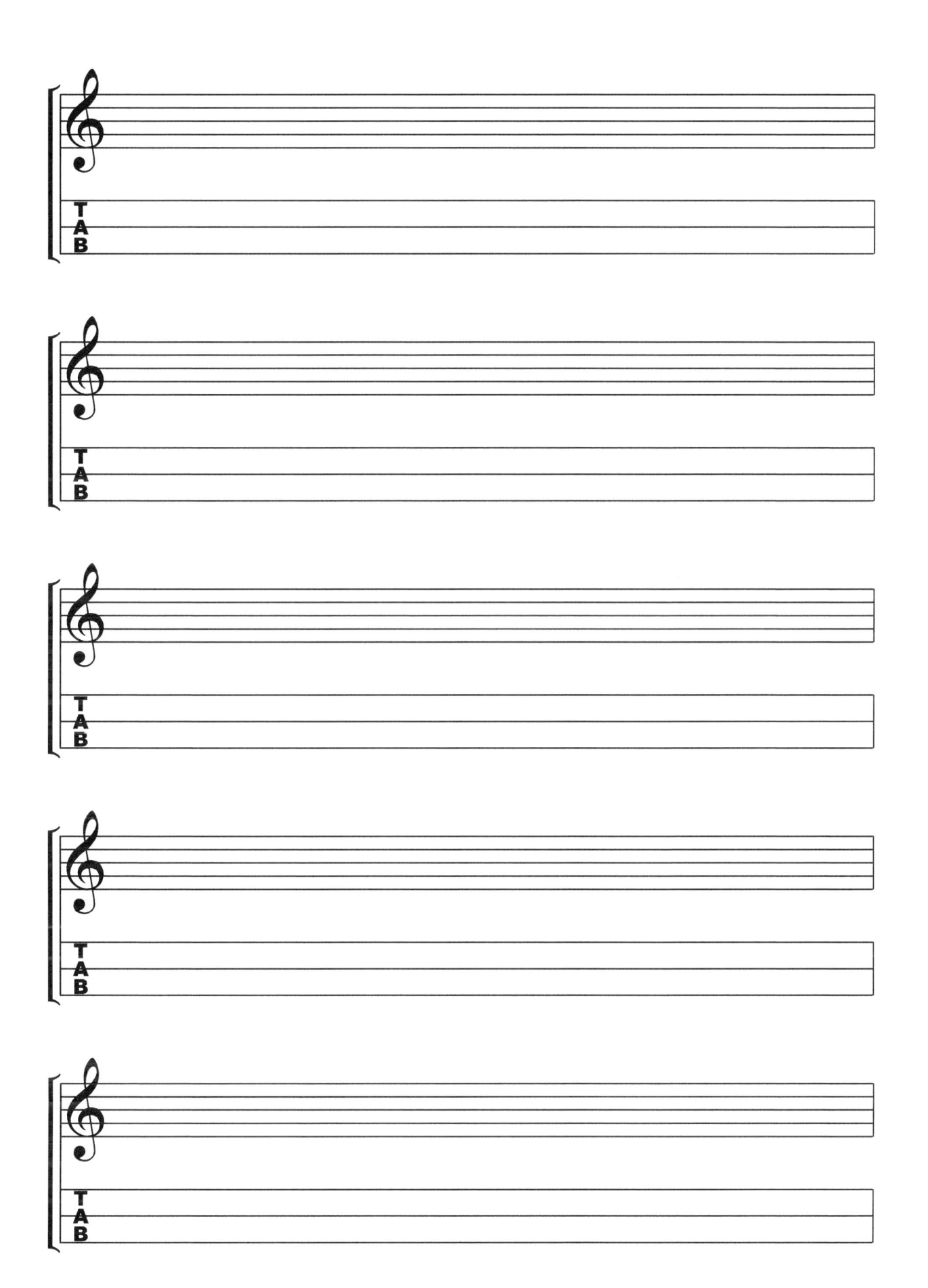

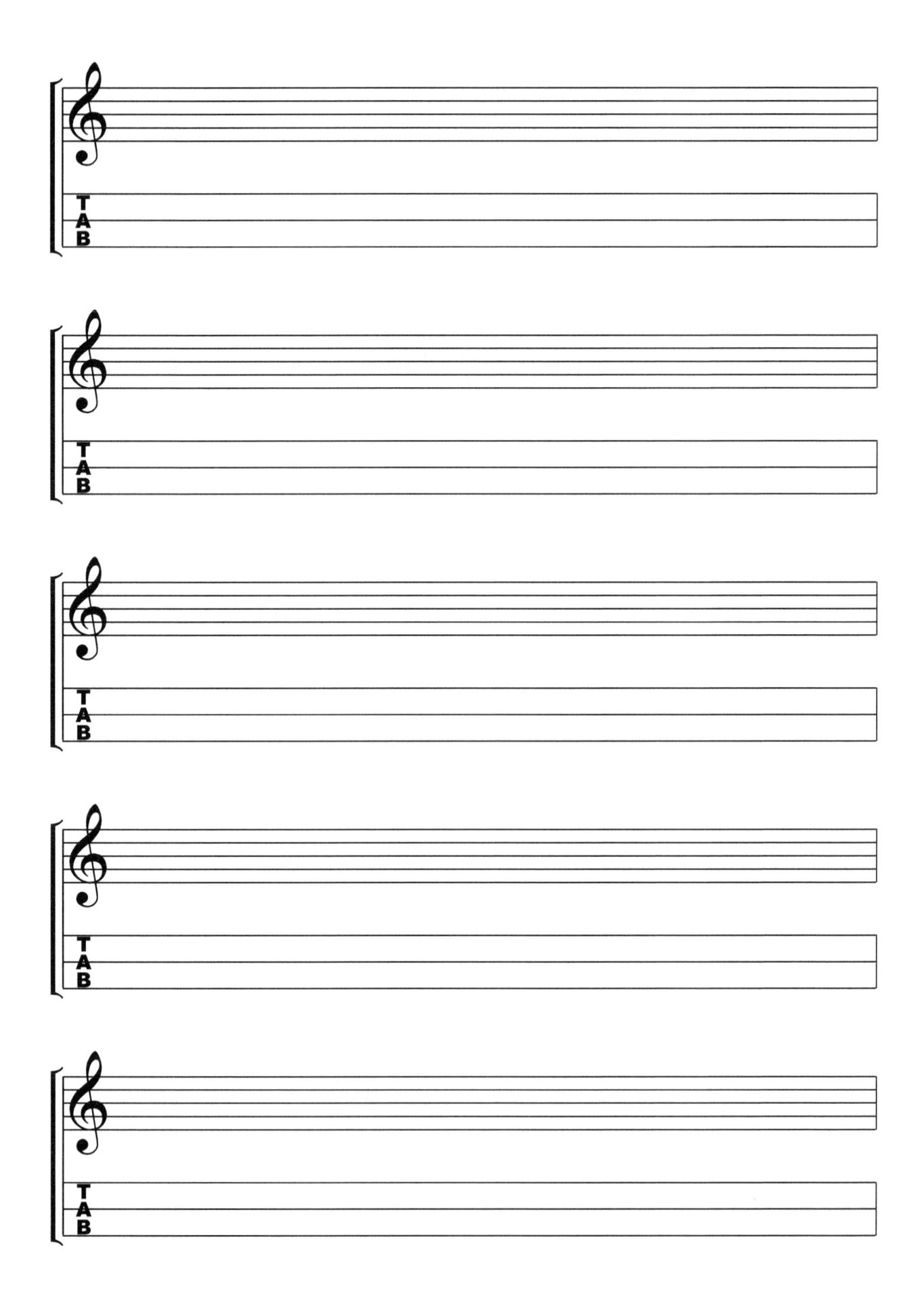

212

217

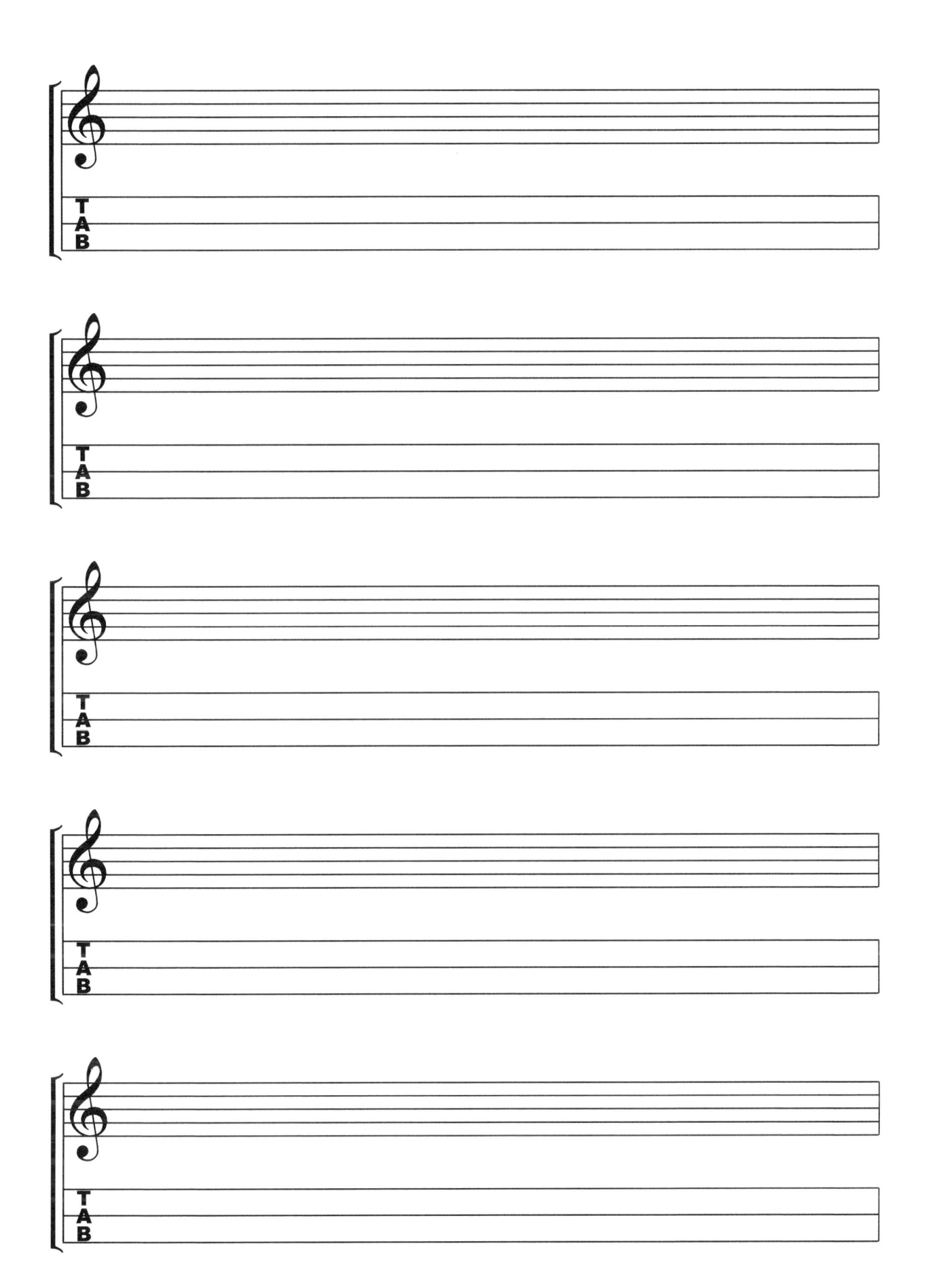

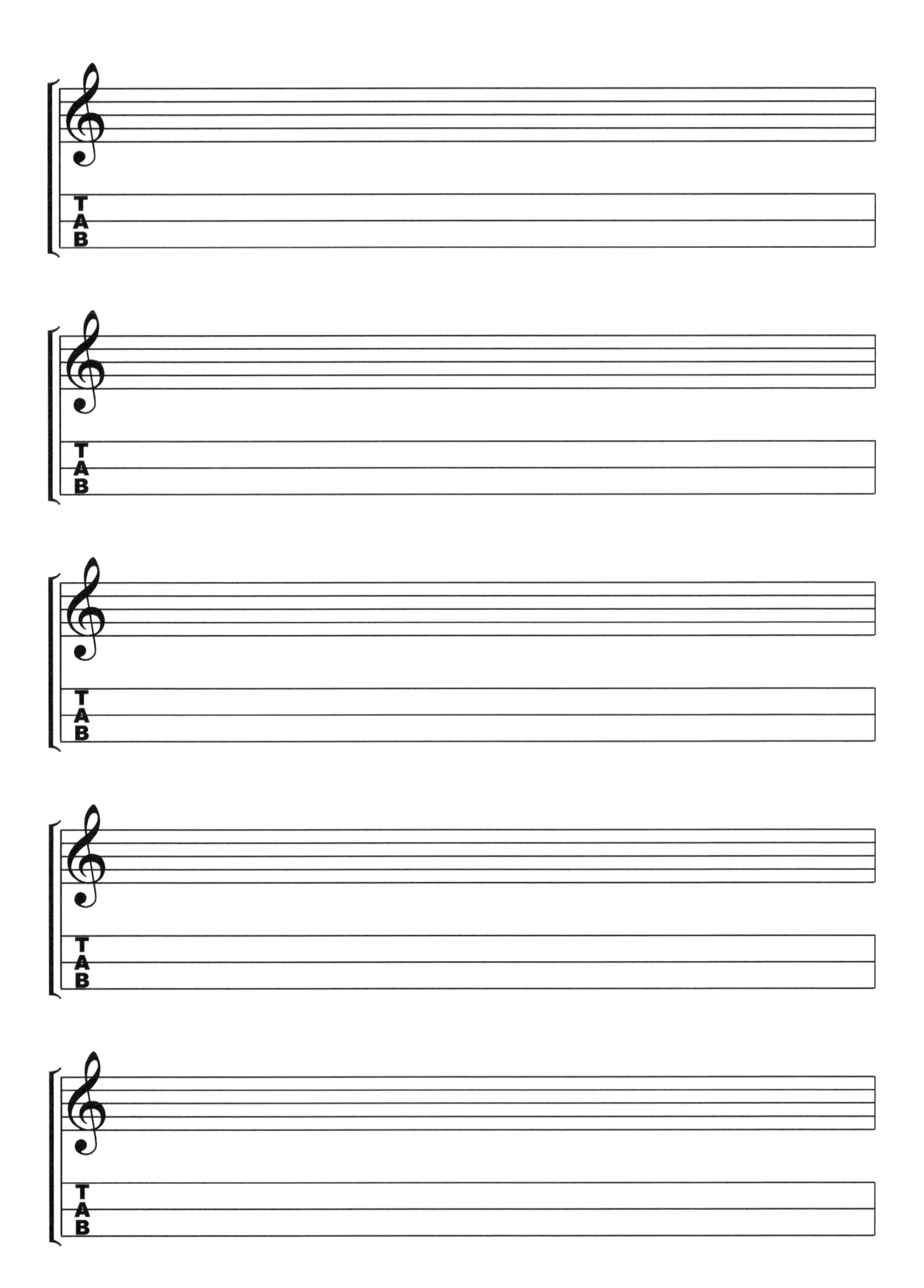

224

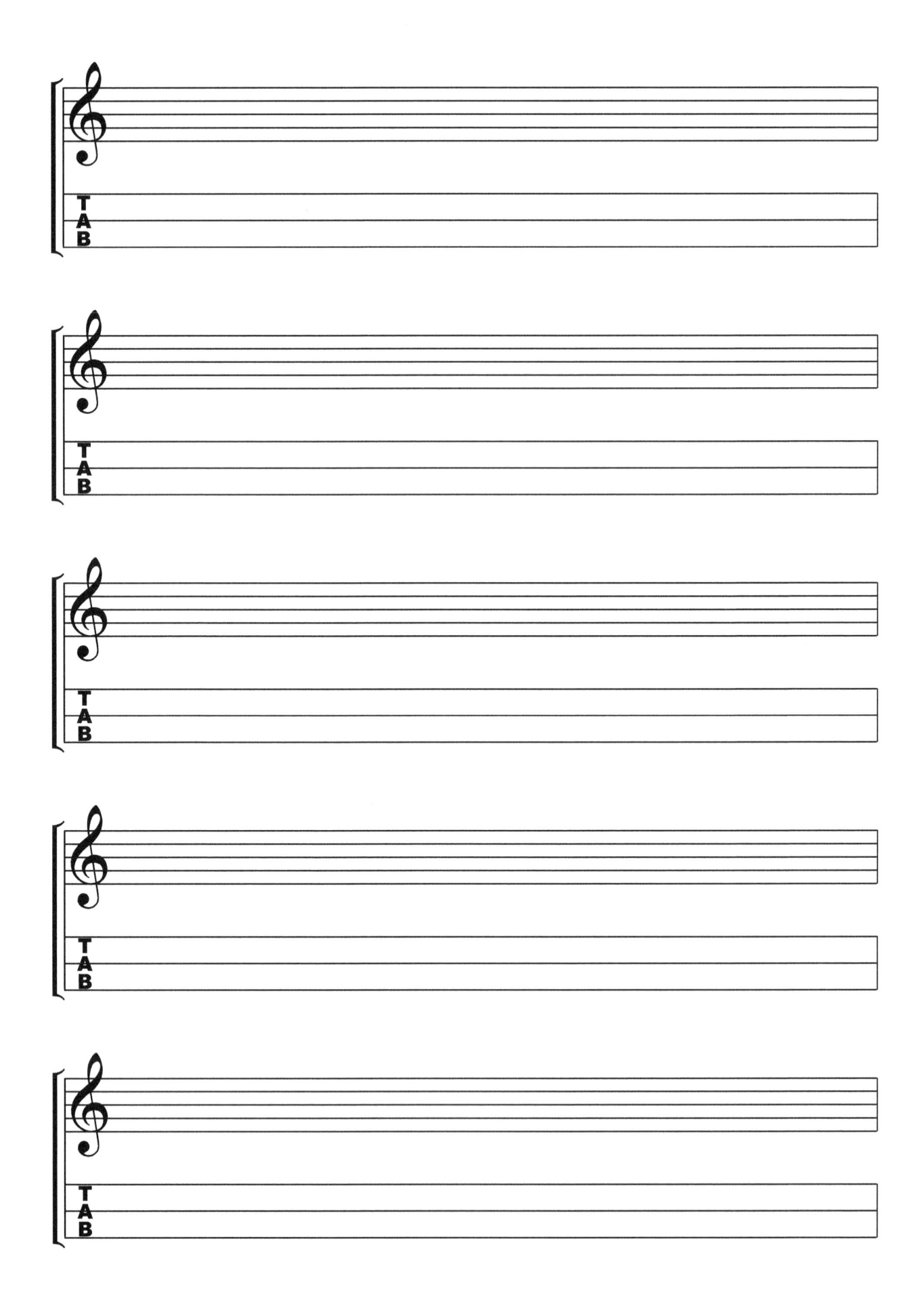

228

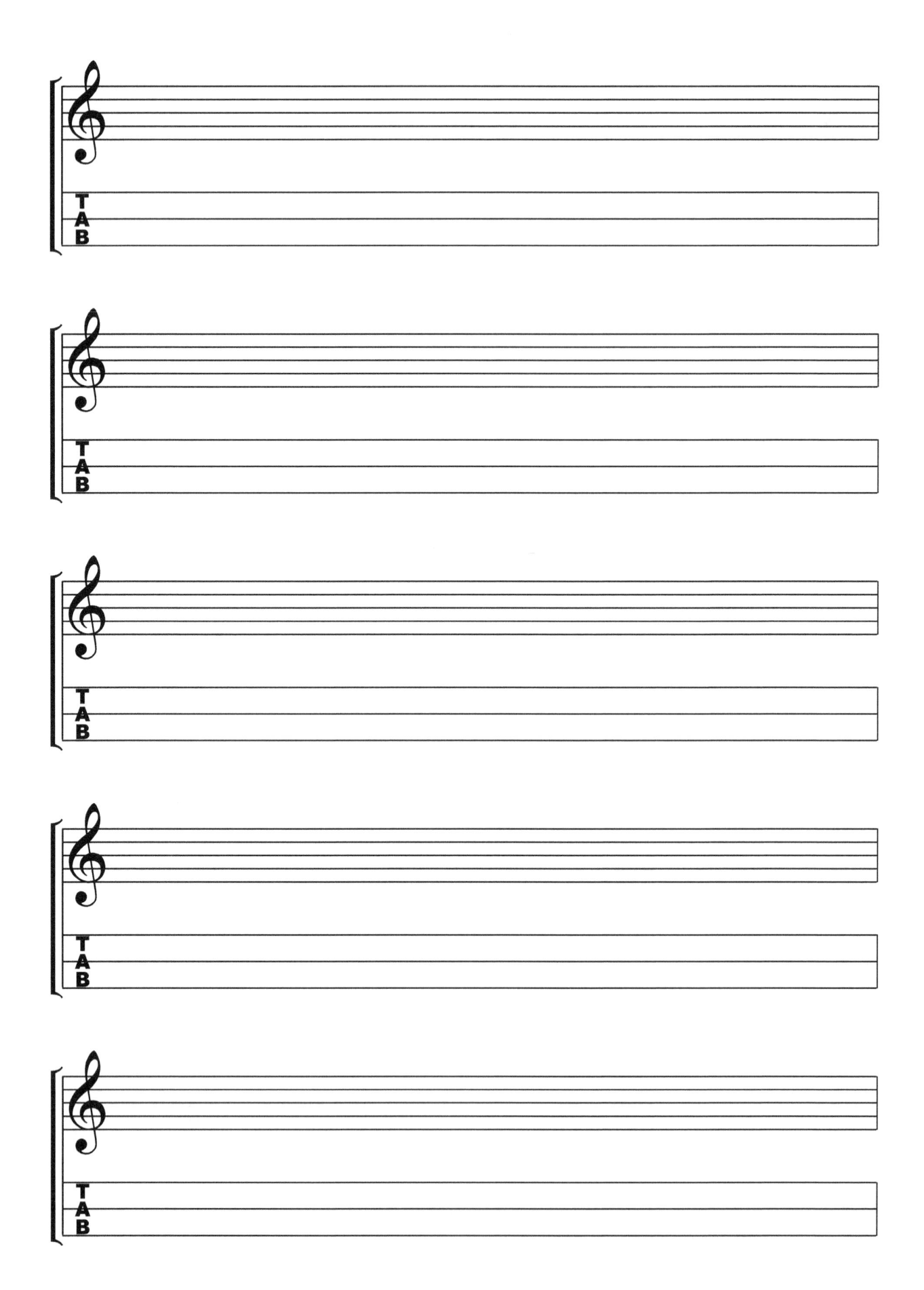

231

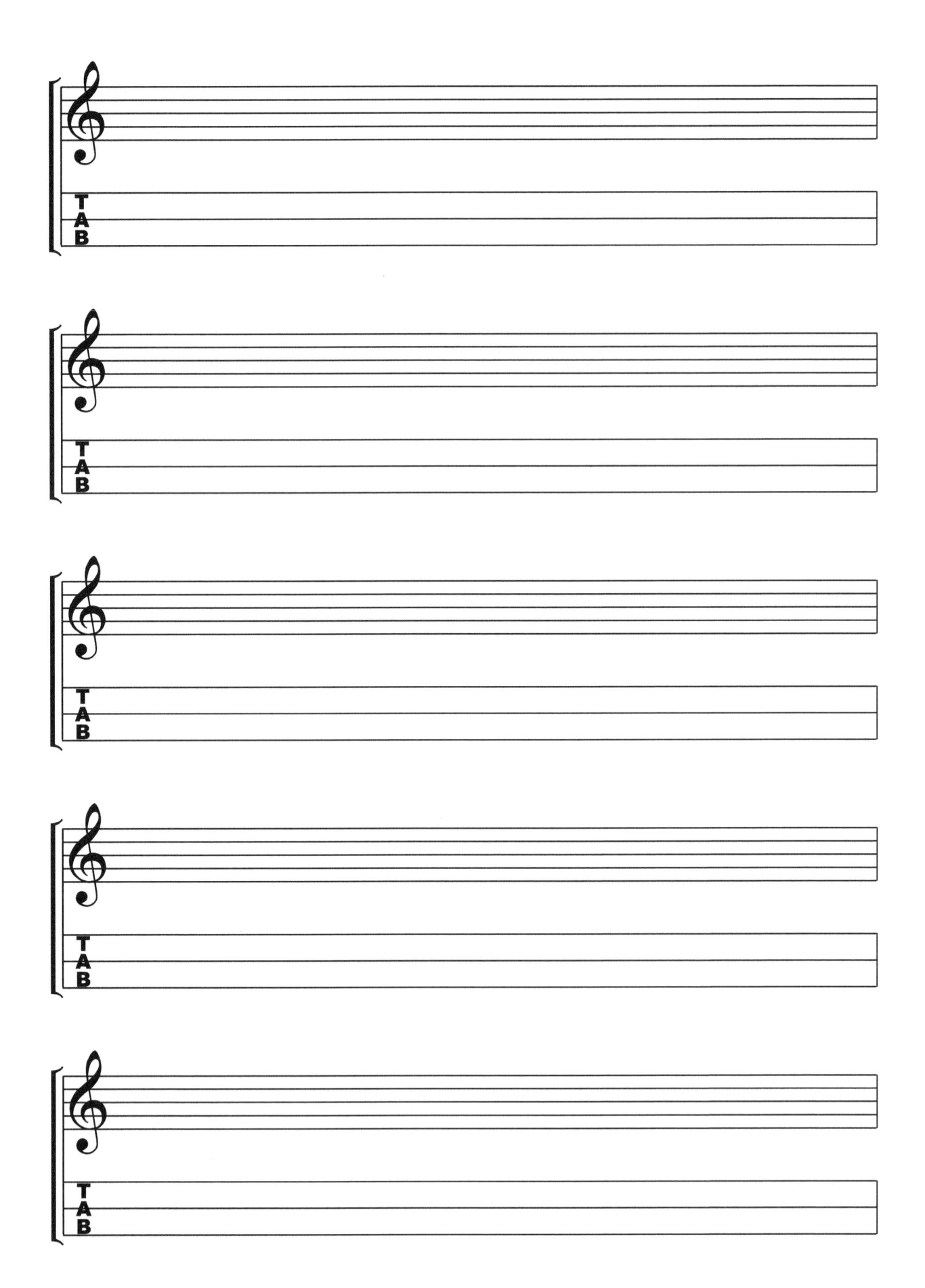

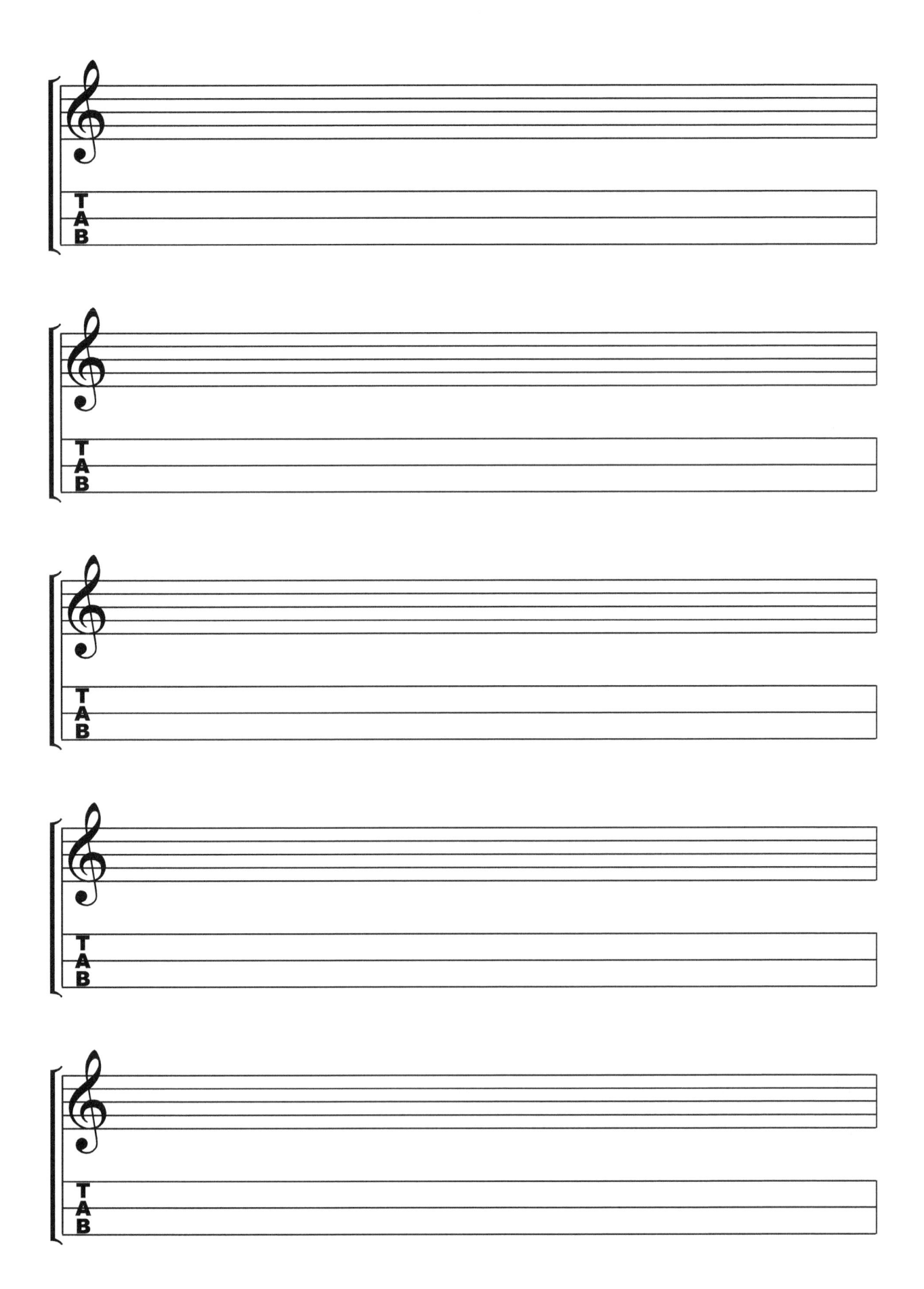

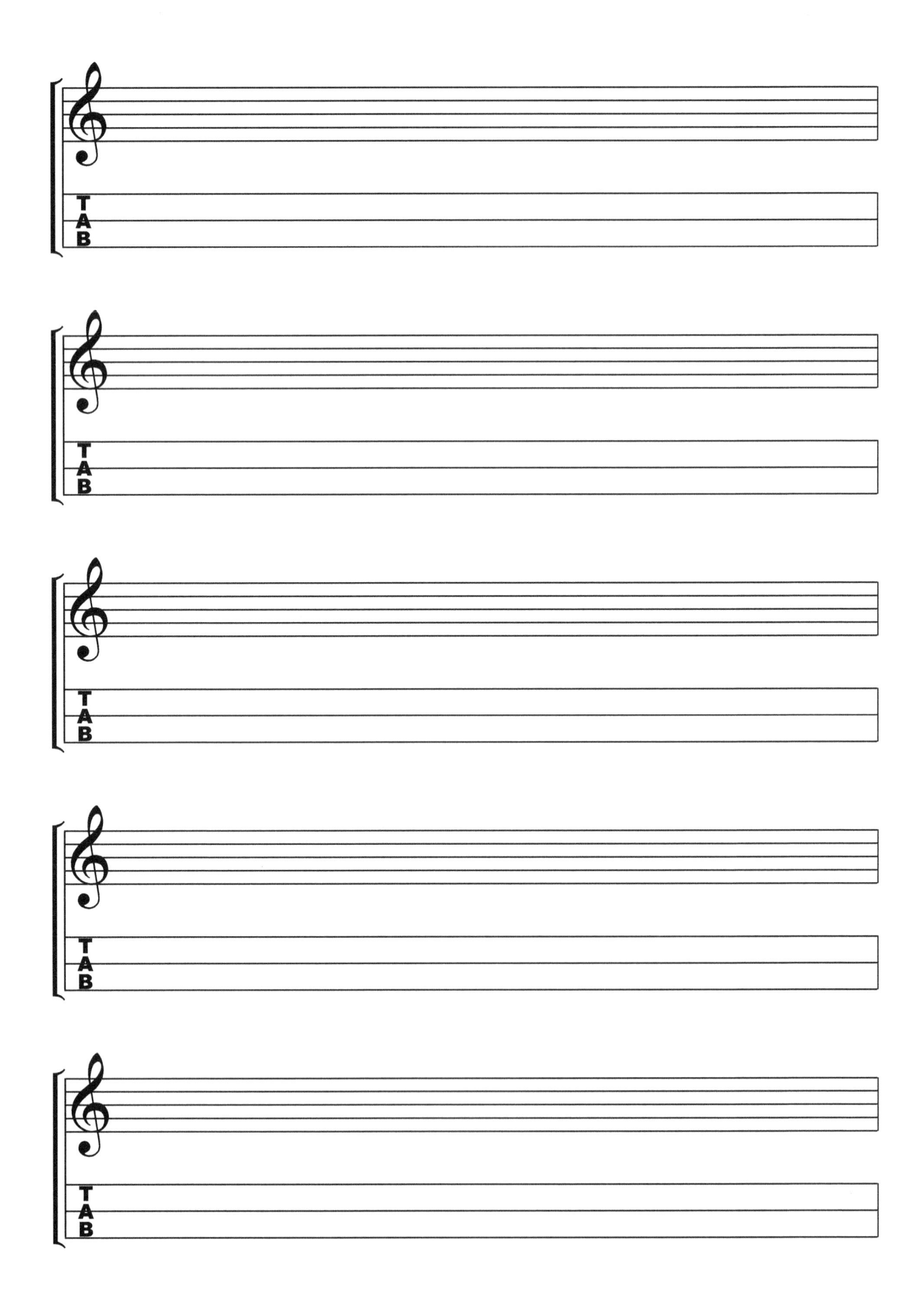

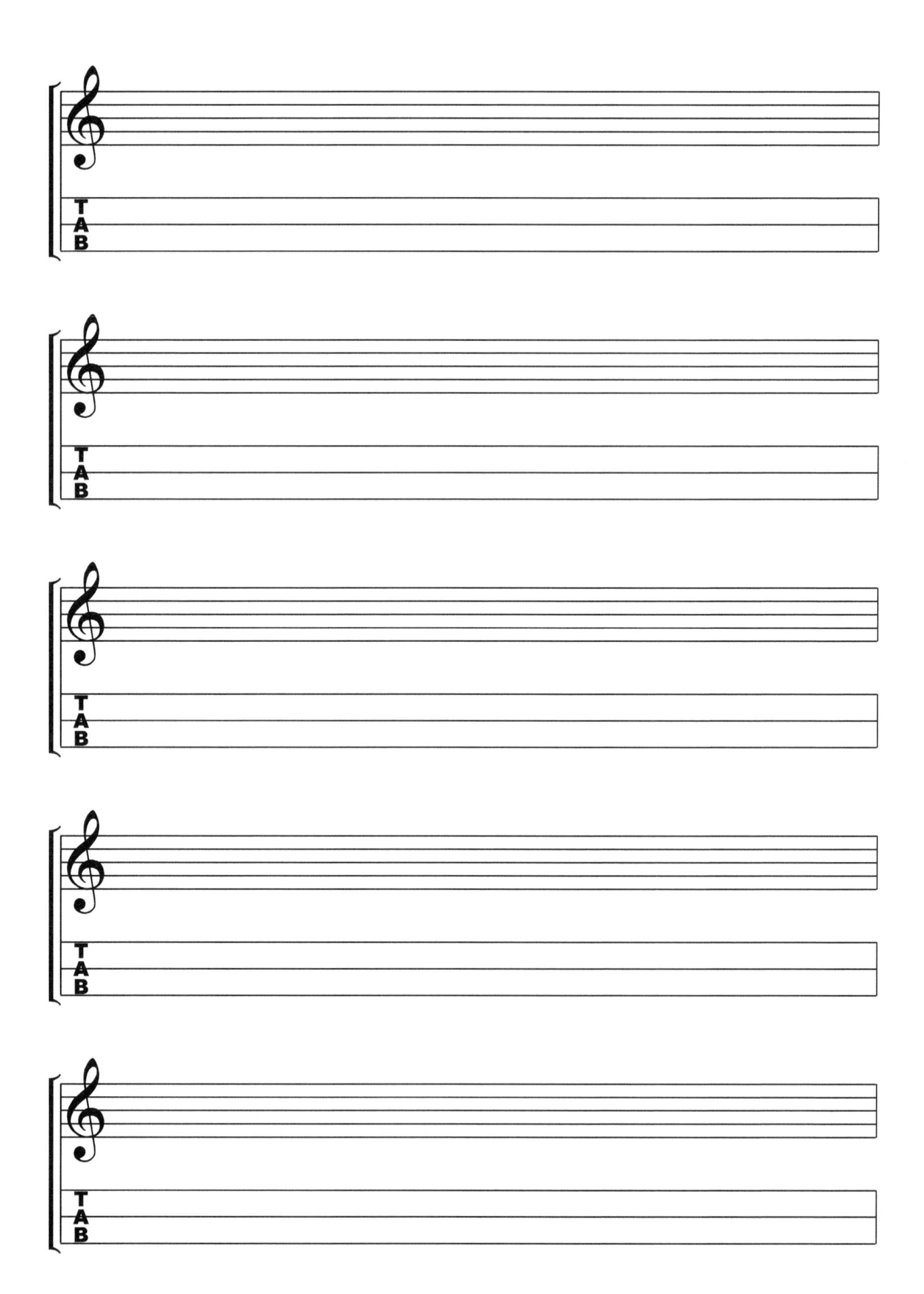

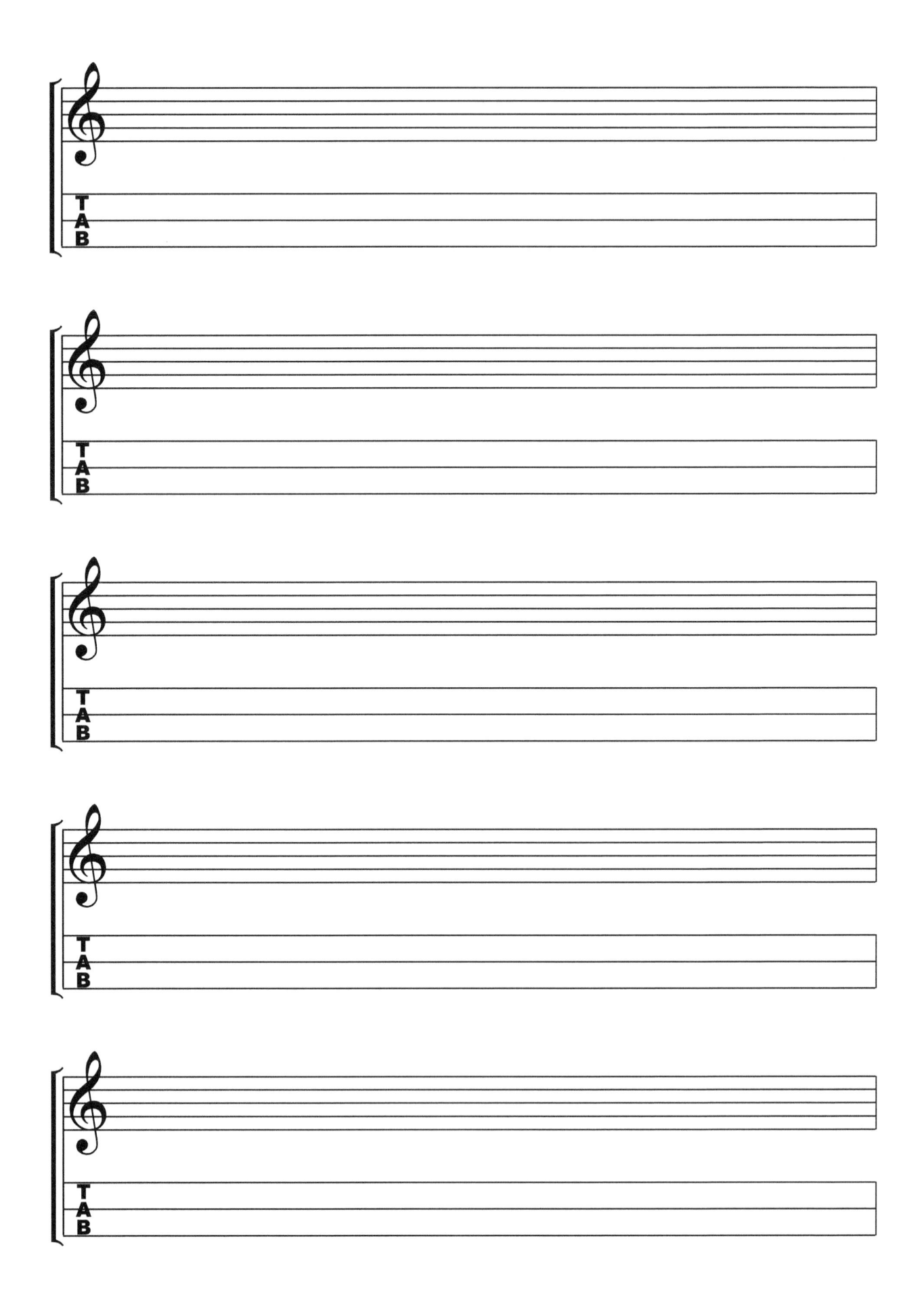

253

254

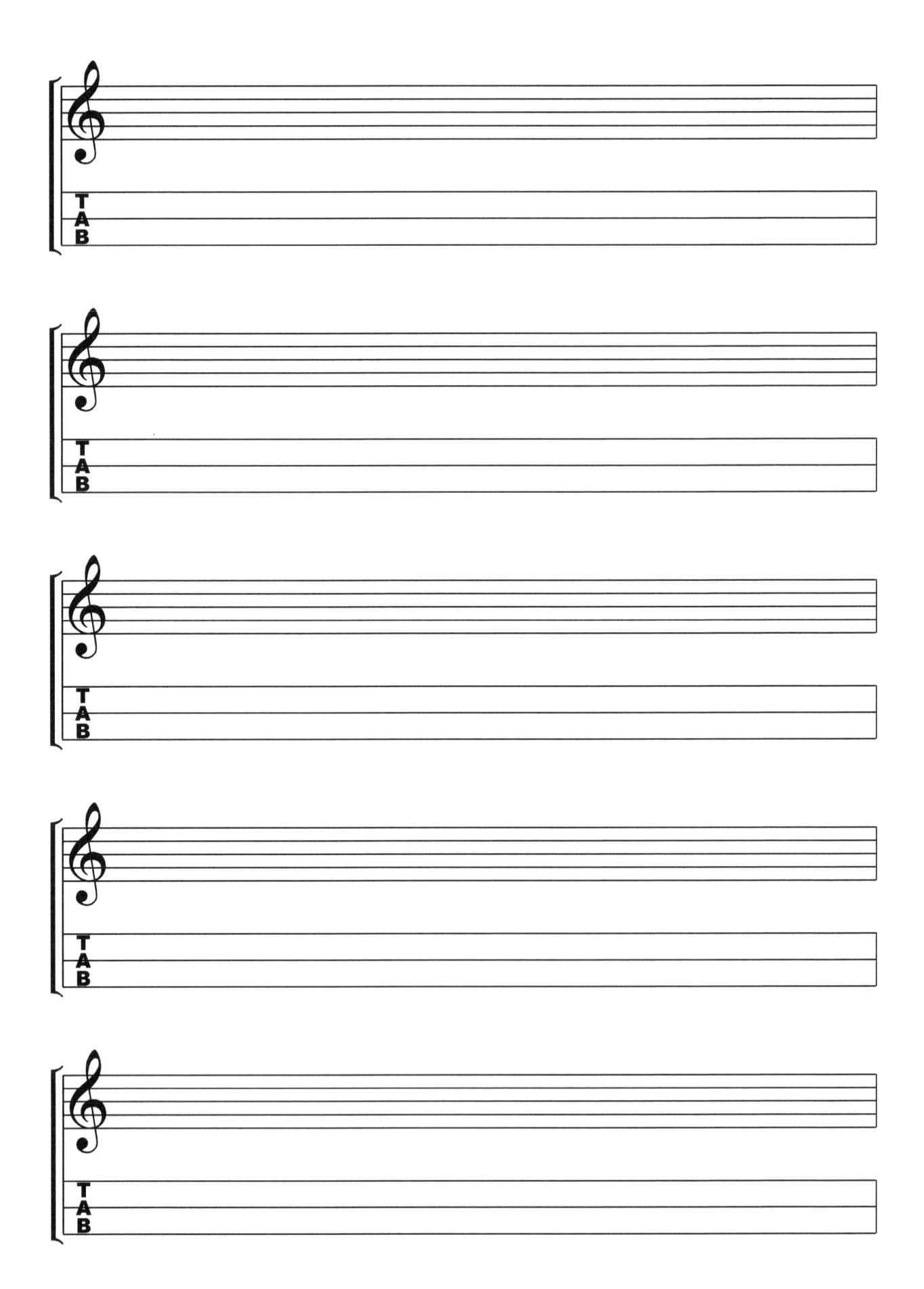

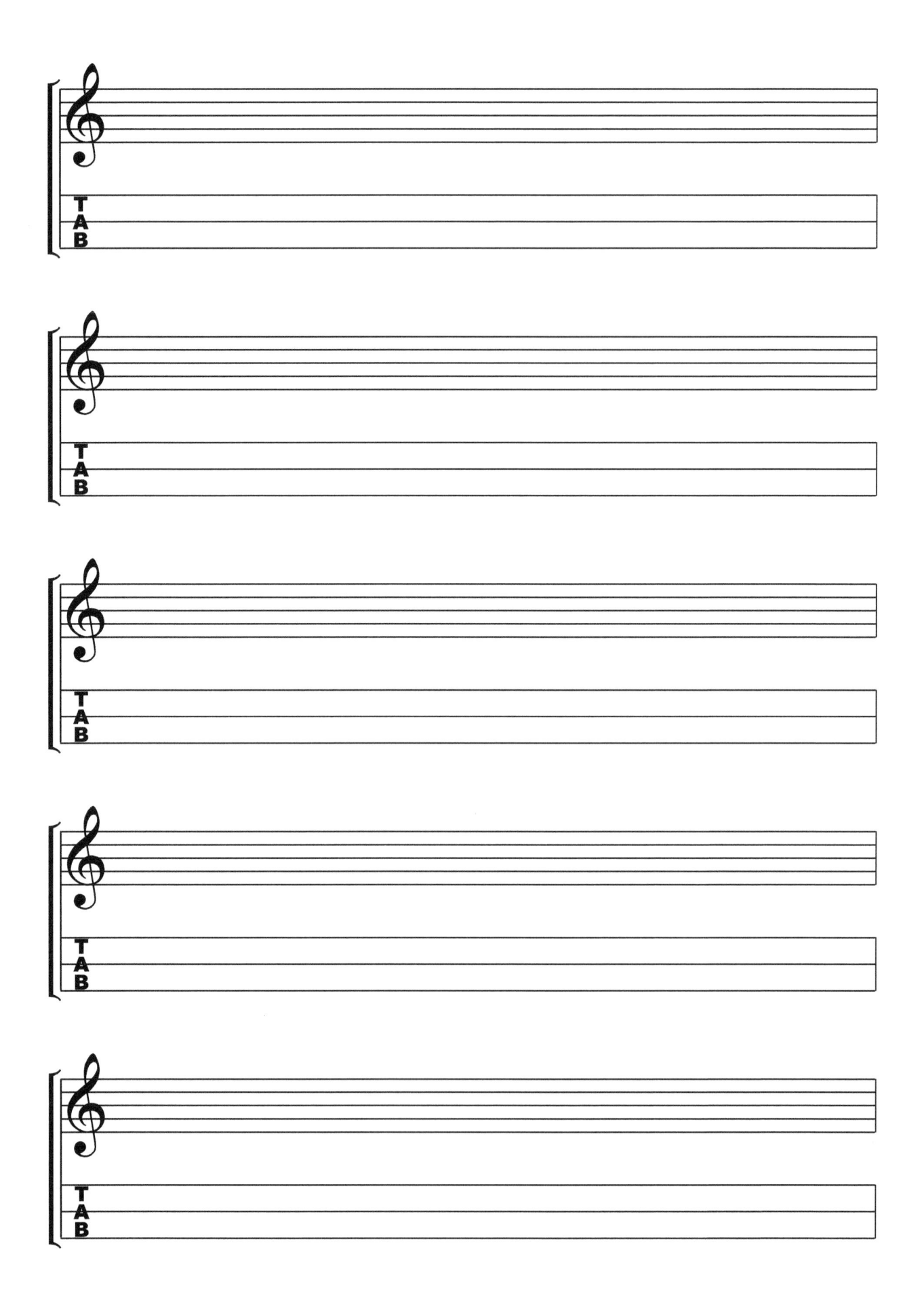

267

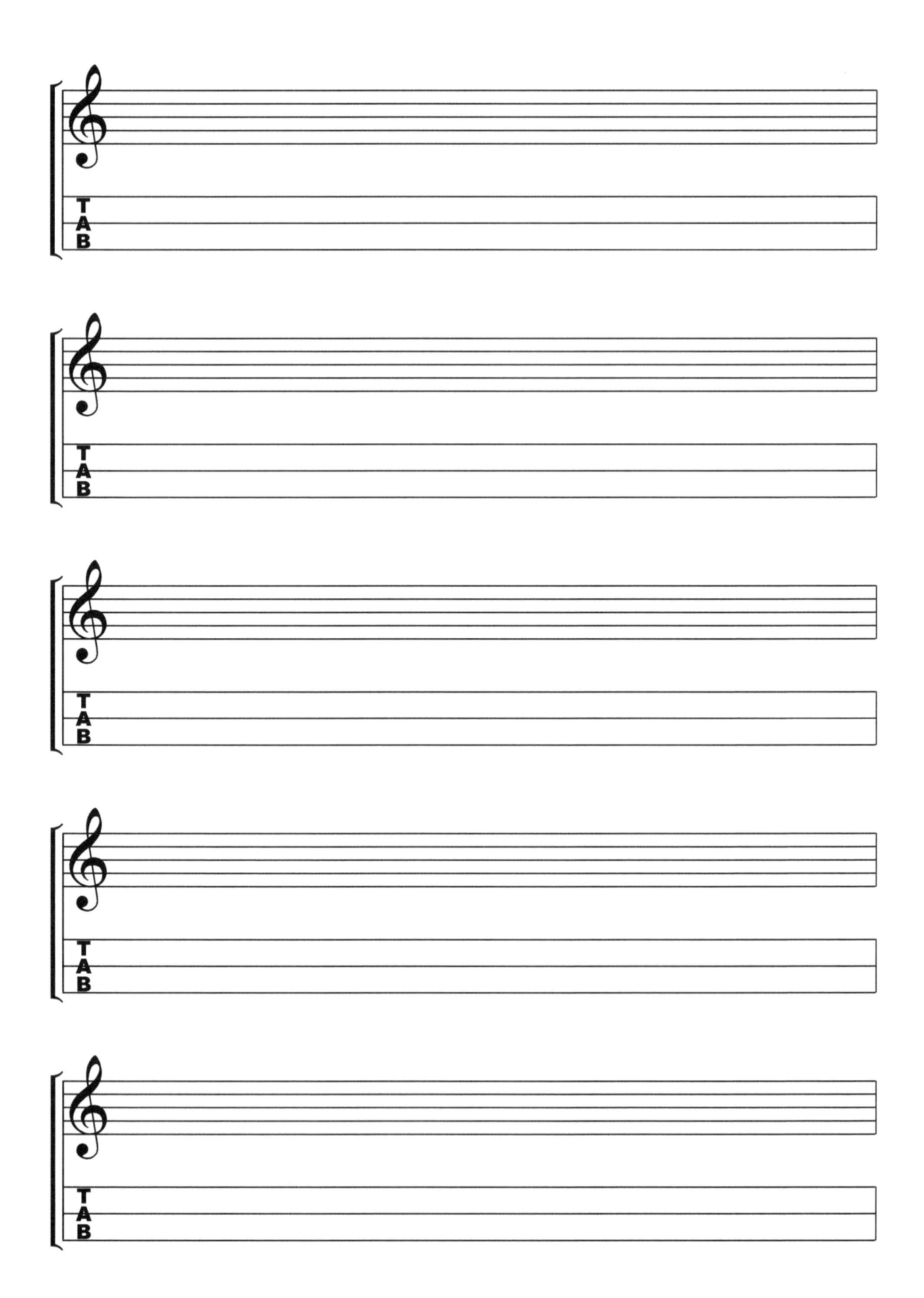

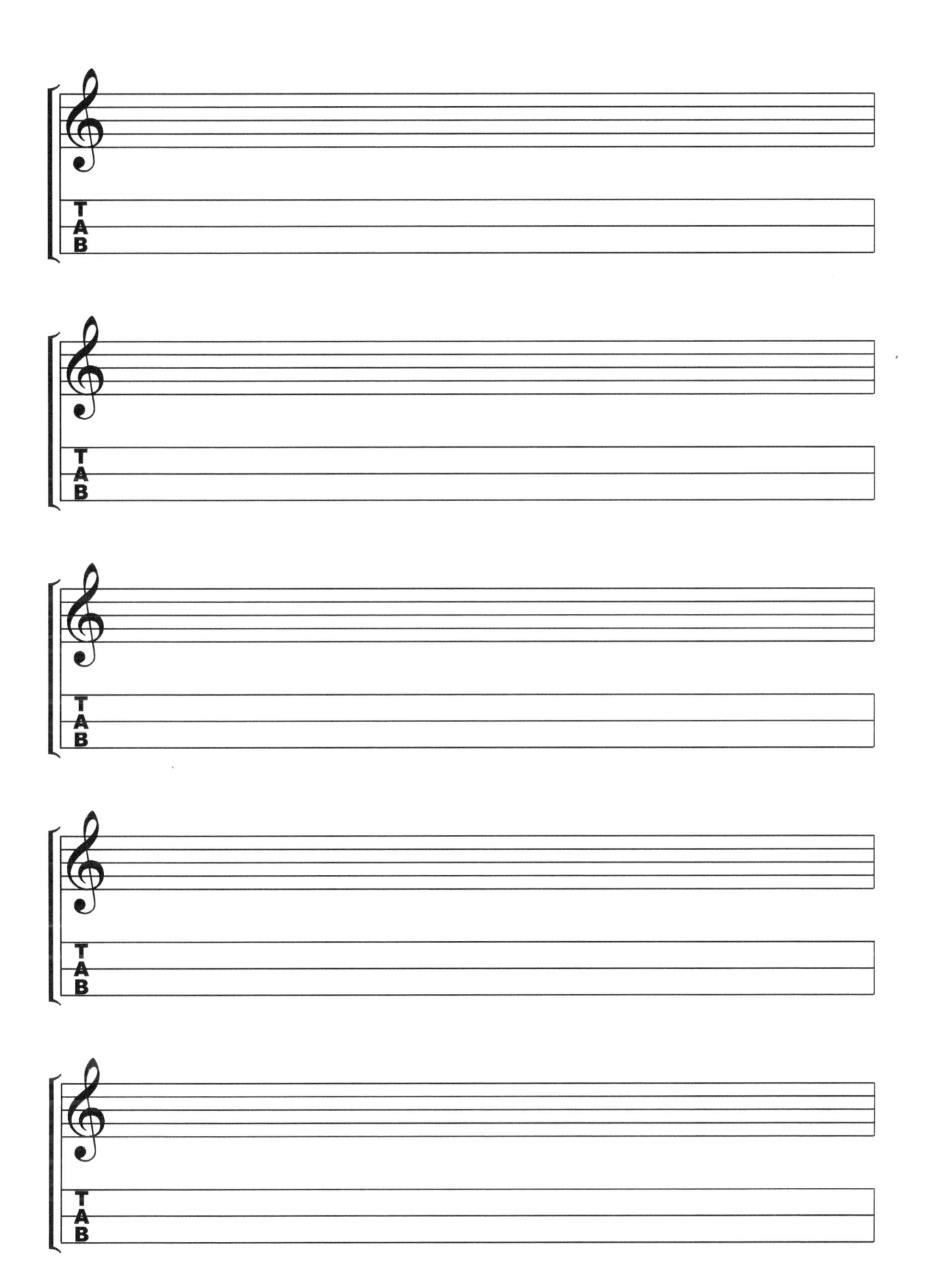

280

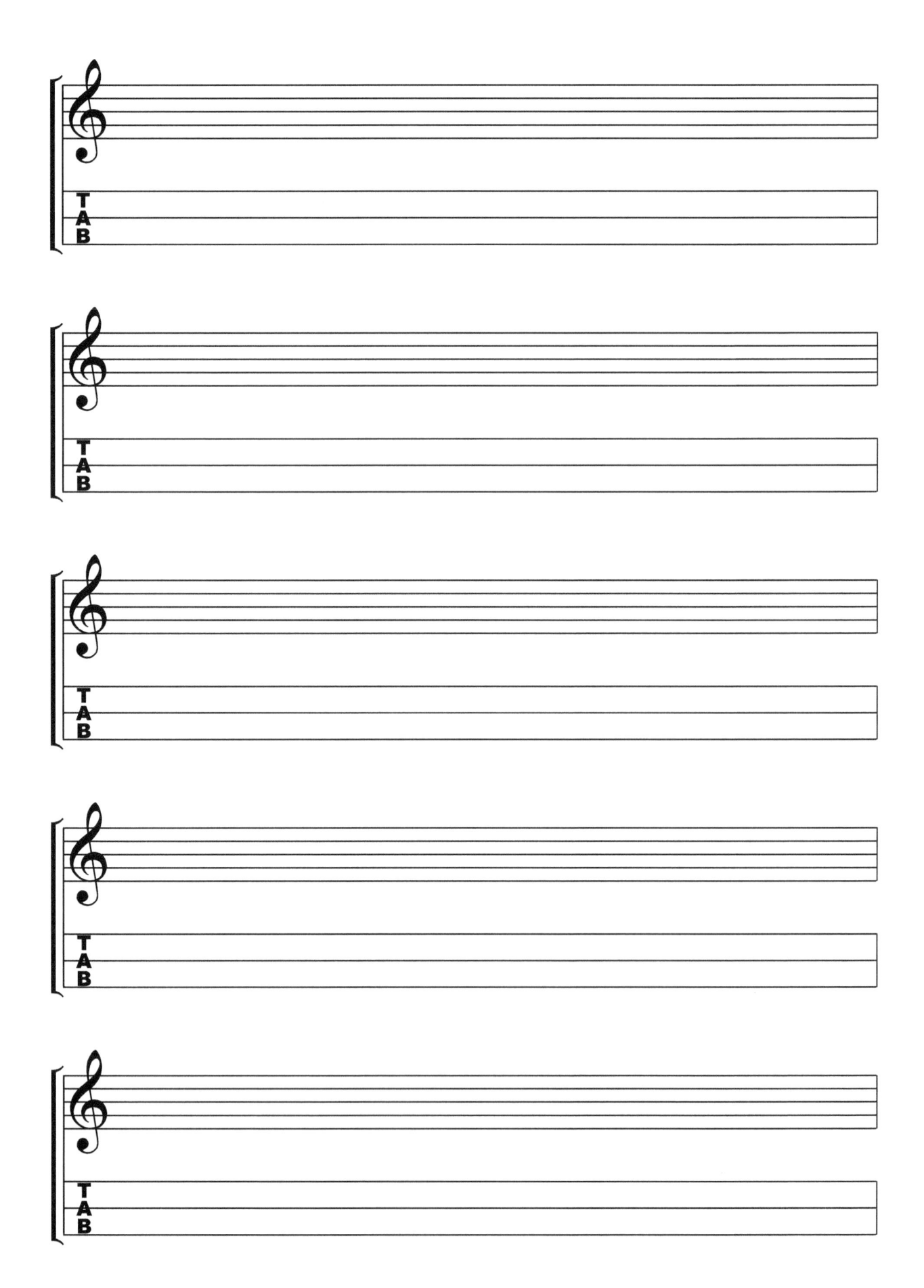

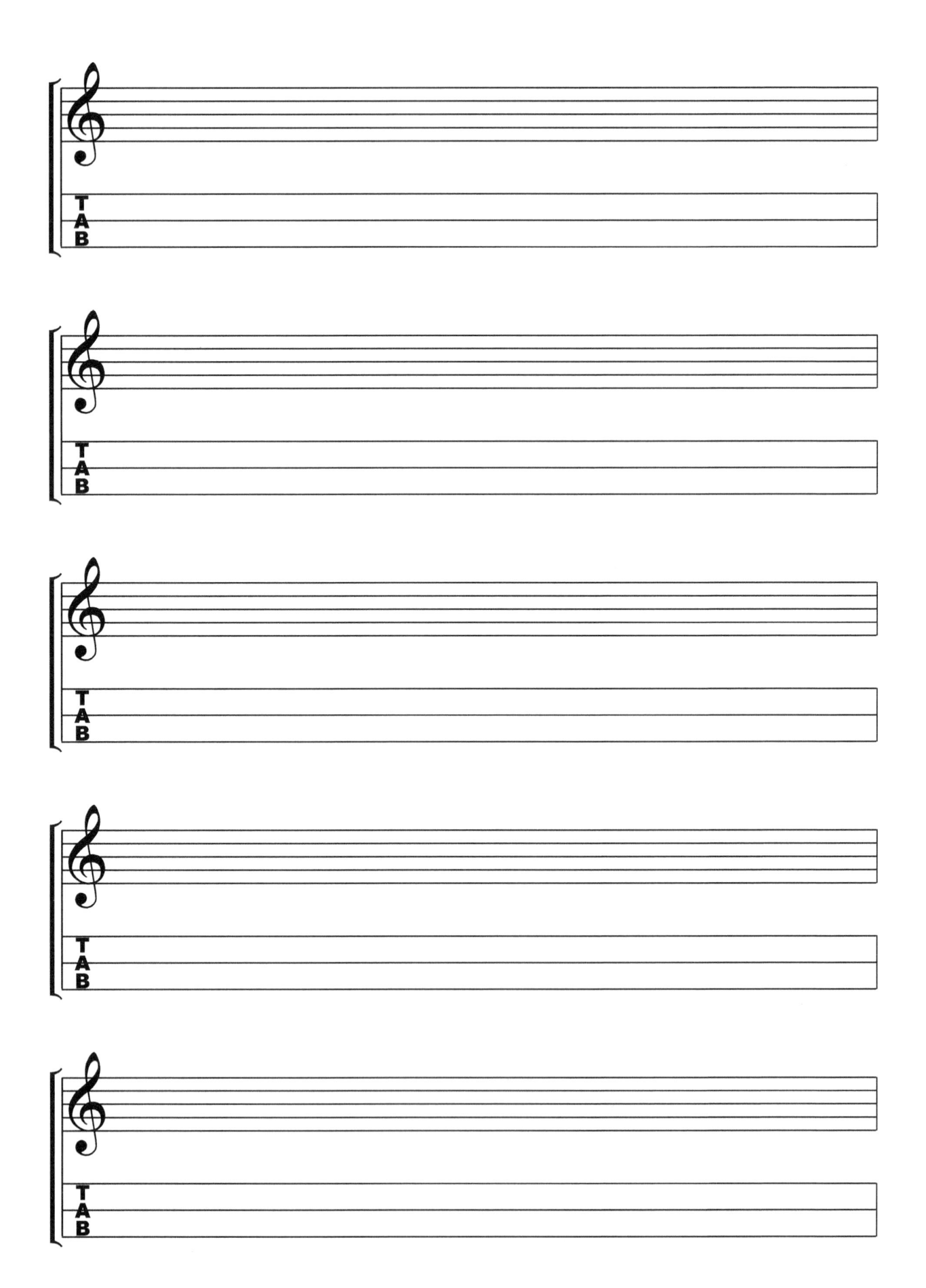

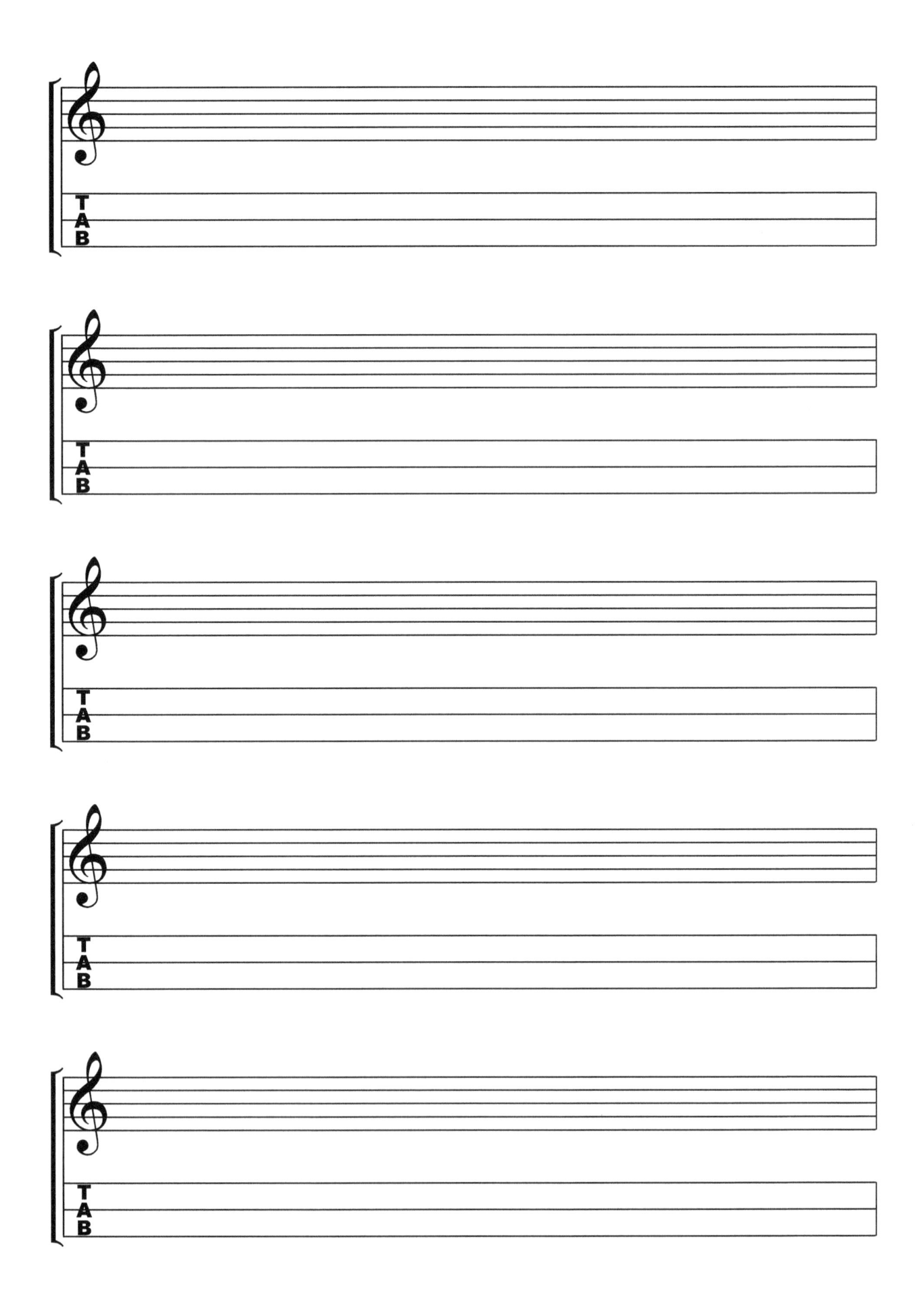

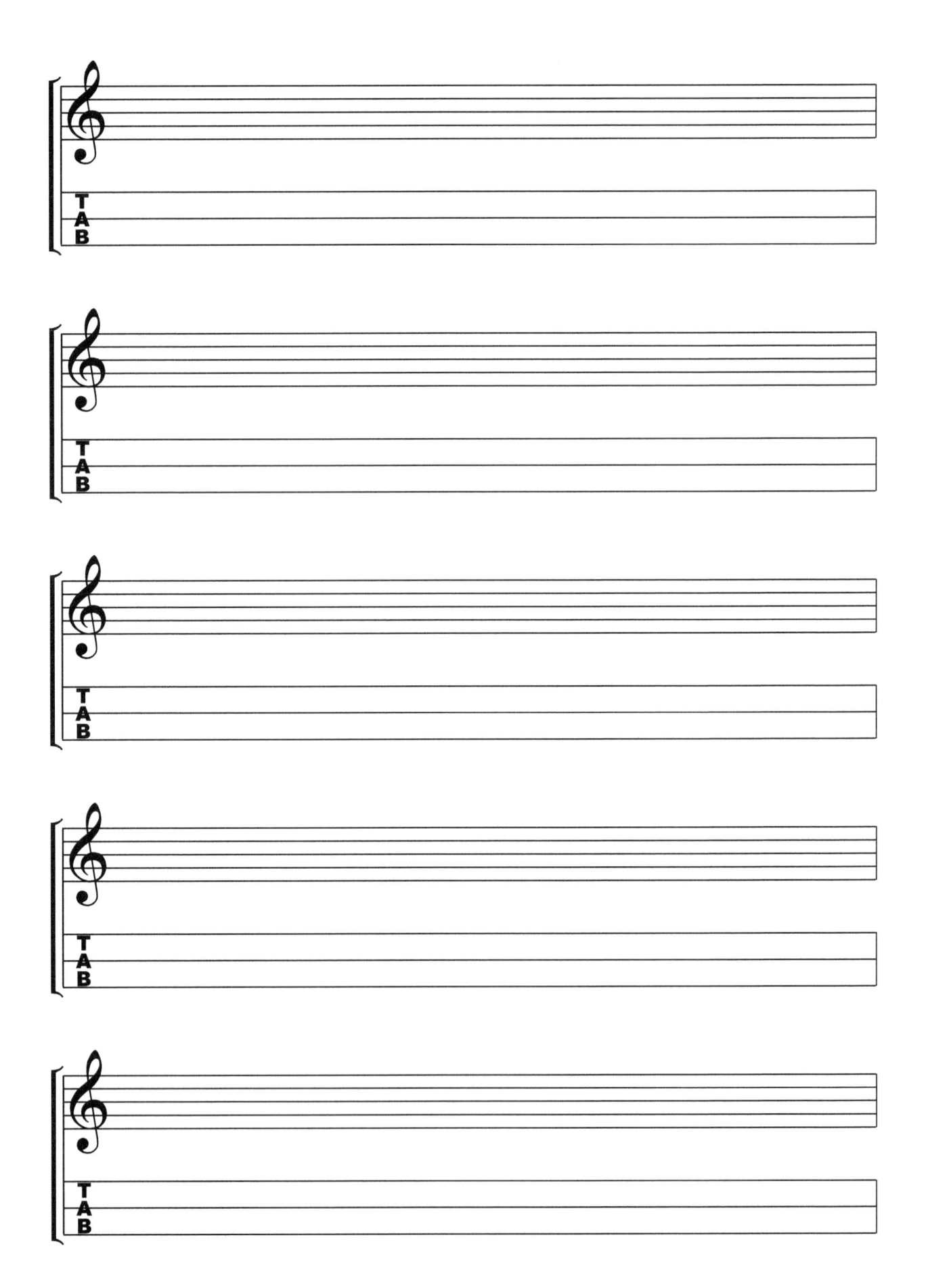

297

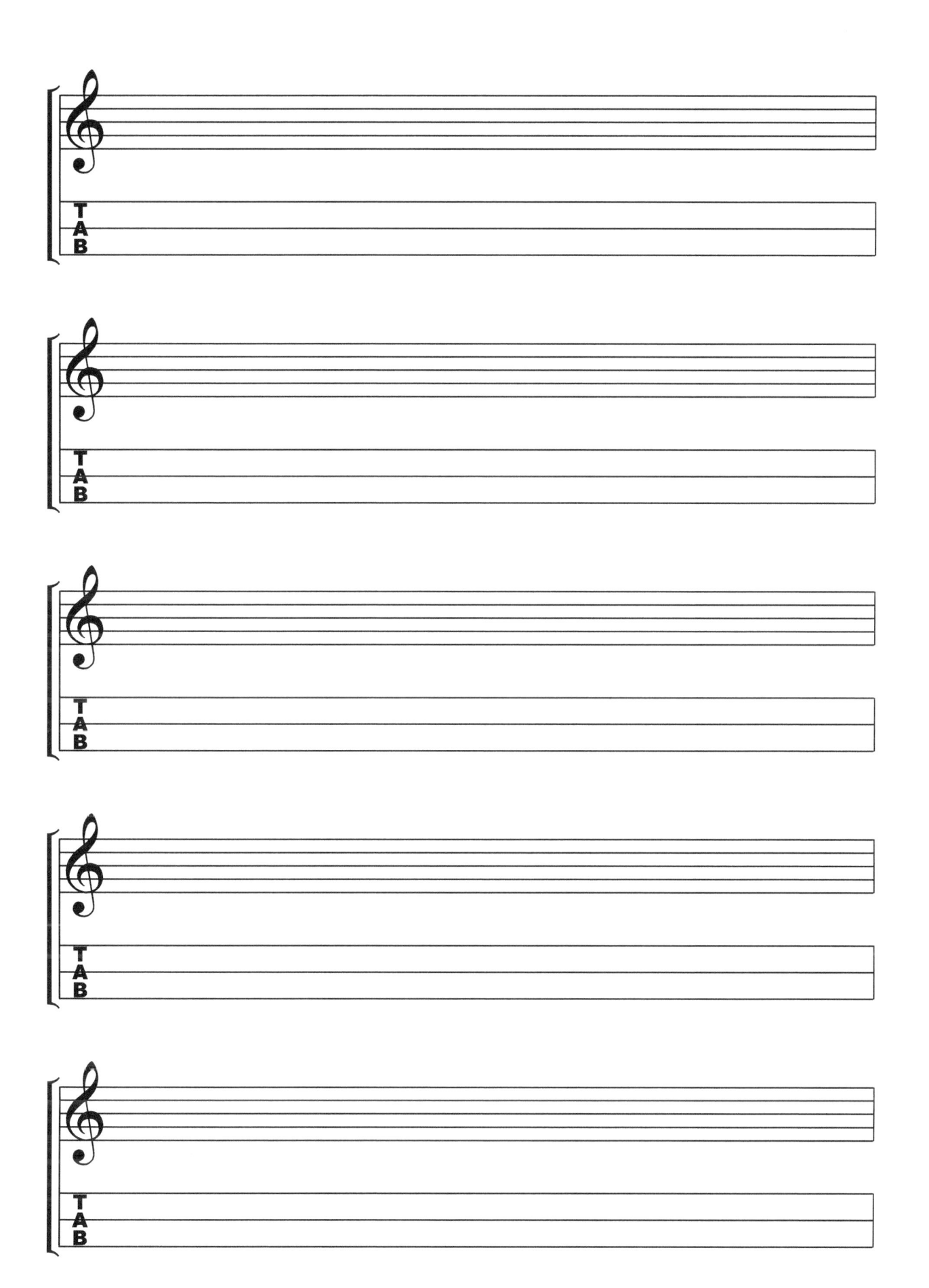

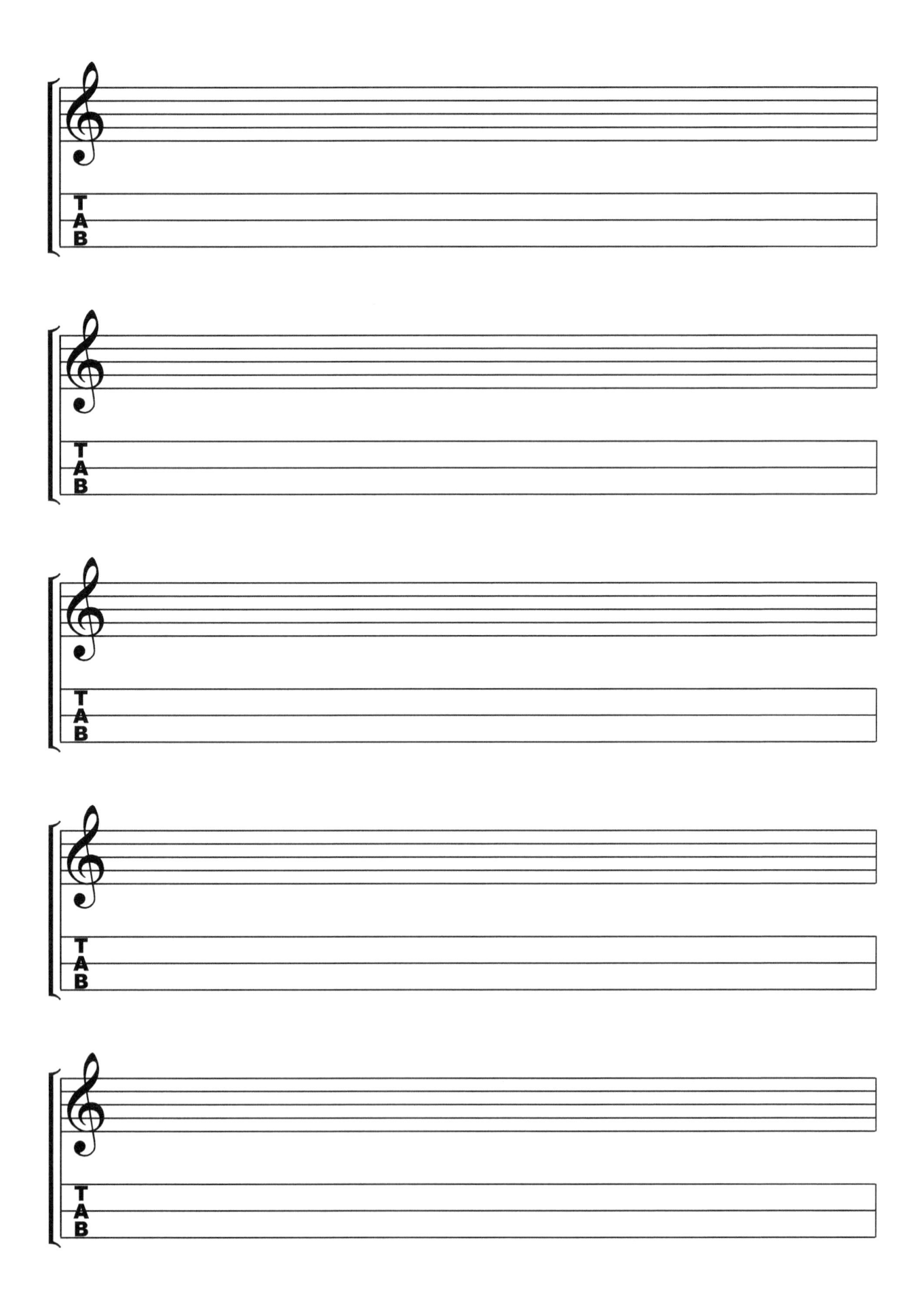

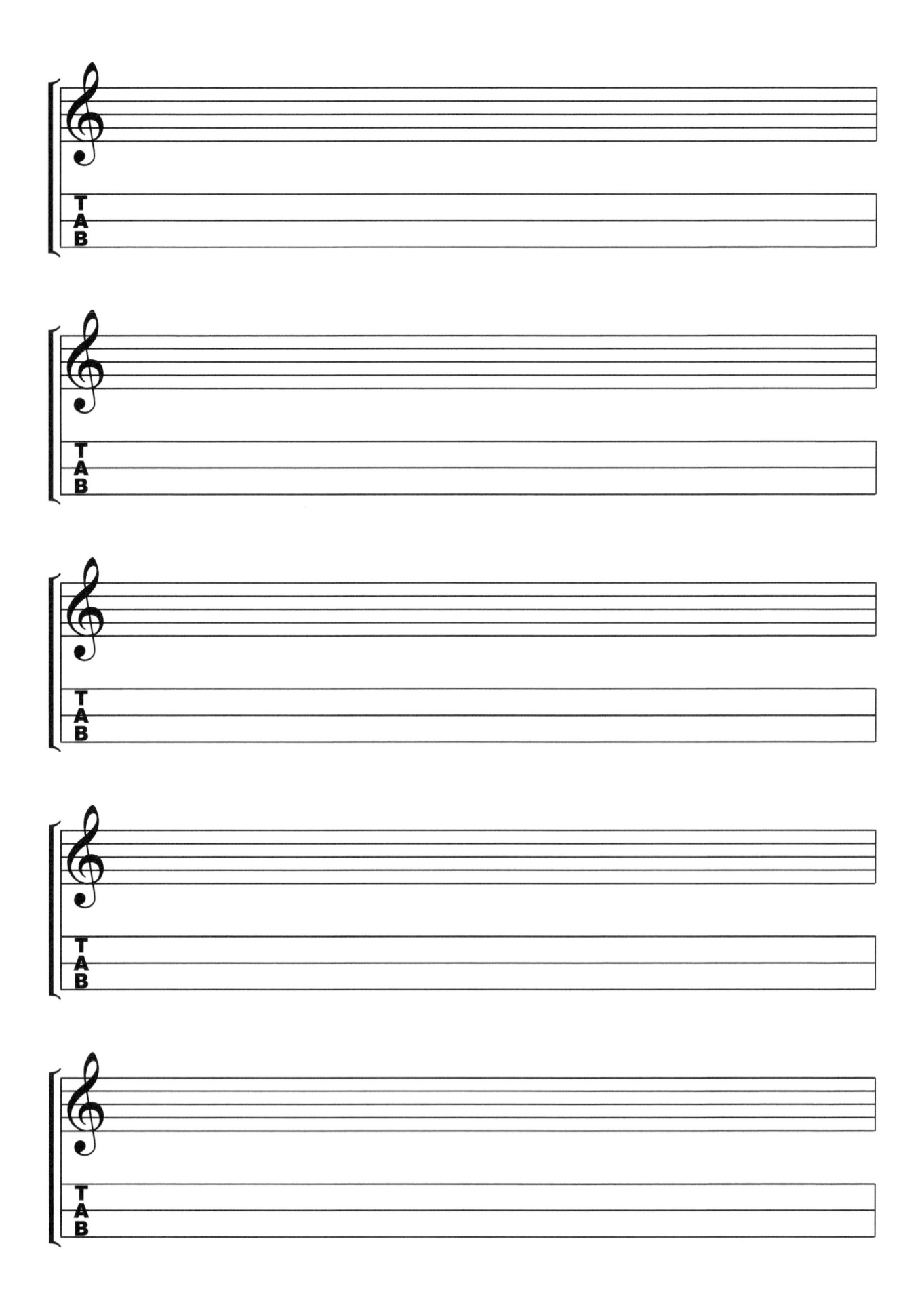

304

Order Form

Bing Futch

                                               Item number

Title	Price	Item number
Method For Beginning Mountain Dulcimer (Book)	$25.00	1310139
Method For Chromatic Mountain Dulcimer (Book)	$25.00	1310144
Getting Started With Mountain Dulcimer (DVD Video)	$15.00	1310088

Richard Ash

Title	Price	Item number
Civil War Songs For Mountain Dulcimer (Book)	$20.00	1310145
Appalachian Tunes For Mountain Dulcimer (Book)	$20.00	1310146
Fret Position Reference Guide, Diatonic (Book)	$25.00	1340001
Fret Position Reference Guide, Chromatic (Book)	$25.00	1390018

Butch Ross

Title	Price	Item number
Chord Book For Mountain Dulcimer, Diatonic (Book)	$20.00	1310147
Chord Book For Mountain Dulcimer, Chromatic (Book)	$20.00	1310149

Stephen Seifert

Title	Price	Item number
Waltzes For Mountain Dulcimer (Book)	$20.00	1310148
Introducing Dulcilele (Book)	$22.00	1390020
Join The Jam, Ukulele Edition (Book)	$28.00	1390019

To order any of these items, you have three great choices:

1) Order online at Folkcraft.com (use the item number shown above to search for your desired product)

2) Order by phone – call Folkcraft Instruments at (800) 433-3655

3) Order by mail – send a check or money order to:

    Folkcraft Instruments, Inc.
    PO Box 302
    Woodburn, IN 46797

FINGERS OF STEEL

Folkcraft INSTRUMENTS

Folkcraft Instruments, Inc.
PO Box 302 / 22133 Main St.
Woodburn, IN 46797

(800) 433-3655 www.Folkcraft.com

Richard Ash is an active dulcimer builder, teacher, and performer.

As the owner of Folkcraft Instruments, he oversees the construction of hundreds of dulcimers each year. As a teacher, he has introduced thousands of people to the dulcimer at festivals and events nationwide. As a performer, he has played everywhere from Carnegie Hall to the local tractor show.

Please visit RichardAsh.com for more information and for booking options.

Folkcraft Instruments

Folkcraft Instruments is one of the oldest and largest builders of acoustic folk instruments in the country. Established in 1968, Folkcraft has a reputation for building long-lived instruments that play in tune. Please visit Folkcraft.com for more information about Folkcraft Instruments.

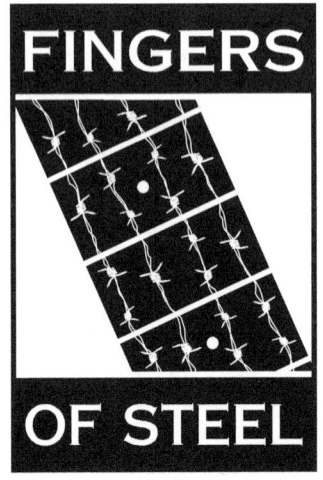

Fingers Of Steel

Fingers Of Steel is a series of books and videos from many of the top artist/instructors in the folk music community. Authors published under the Fingers Of Steel imprint include: Stephen Seifert, Butch Ross, Richard Ash, and Bing Futch.

There is an order form at the end of this book with a complete listing of all Fingers Of Steel publications.

CPSIA information can be obtained
at www.ICGtesting.com
Printed in the USA
LVHW060159190220
647432LV00017B/237